Workbook/Study Guide

to accompany

Managerial Accounting

Ray H. Garrison
Professor of Accounting
Brigham Young University

1985
Fourth Edition

Business Publications, Inc.
Plano, Texas

Preface

To The Student

This study guide has been prepared for your use as a student in the study of managerial accounting. It is designed to supplement the fourth edition of *Managerial Accounting: Concepts for Planning, Control, Decision Making,* by Ray H. Garrison. The purposes of the study guide are:

1. To provide suggestions for the study of chapter material.
2. To summarize the essential points in each chapter, thus making it possible to review chapter material quickly, particularly before examinations.
3. To test your knowledge of chapter material by means of a series of *self-test* questions and exercises. Answers to these questions and exercises are provided immediately following the questions and exercises themselves in order to give you immediate feedback and to point out areas that may need additional study.

Each chapter in the study guide begins with a brief section titled *Chapter Study Suggestions.* These study suggestions relate to the corresponding textbook chapter and will help you in your initial reading of the chapter material. Immediately following these study suggestions, a chapter outline is provided which highlights the key points and concepts discussed in the text. The purpose of this outline is to help you review the chapter material before attempting to complete the self-test questions and exercises provided for each chapter in the study guide. The self-test questions and exercises consist of true-false questions, multiple-choice questions, completion statements, and short exercises. This self-test material is designed to both measure and reinforce your understanding.

The way in which this study guide is used may differ from student to student; however, we would recommend the following approach:

1. Before reading the chapter in your textbook, read the *Chapter Study Suggestions* contained at the beginning of the corresponding chapter in the study guide.
2. Study the textbook chapter.
3. Study the outline contained in the *Chapter Highlights* section of the study guide. If you encounter any statements or comments that you do not understand, refer to the textbook for a more detailed discussion of the topic.
4. Work the review questions and exercises contained in the study guide, and then compare your answers to those given in the study guide. If you find something you don't understand, refer to the textbook for help.
5. Work the homework exercises and/or problems assigned by your instructor.

Remember, the study guide is not intended as a substitute for the textbook. Rather, its purpose is to *supplement* the textbook and to serve as an *aid* to learning.

The author welcomes suggestions and comments from users.

Ray H. Garrison

Contents

Chapter 1

Managerial Accounting—
A Perspective

Chapter Study Suggestions

As its title indicates, the purpose of this chapter is to provide a perspective of managerial accounting. The chapter describes the work that managers do and the kinds of information they need in order to do this work effectively. Study the section titled "The Work of Management" carefully; it contains a number of key concepts which carry on through the book. Also pay particular note to the similarities between organizations discussed in the chapter.

Many new terms are introduced in the chapter. Study these terms with care, and be sure you understand *how* the terms are used in the chapter discussion.

In order to ease your transition from financial accounting to managerial accounting, be sure you understand the points made in the "Comparison of Financial and Managerial Accounting" section near the end of the chapter.

CHAPTER HIGHLIGHTS AND STUDY GUIDE

A.   An organization is a group of people united together for a common objective or purpose. The objective(s) of an organization are set by its managers, through strategic planning. Strategic planning occurs in two phases: 1) deciding on the product/service to produce/render, and 2) deciding on the best way to market the desired product/service.

B.   The work of management centers around the thing to be managed—the organization. Four broad functions are involved in the manager's work:

1.   Planning, which involves deciding on the actions to be taken in order to achieve the organization's objectives.

2.   Organizing and directing, which involve putting the organization's resources together effectively and overseeing day-to-day activities.

3.   Controlling, which involves the obtaining of feedback to ensure that all parts of the organization are following the plans which have been set and approved.

4.   Decision making, which involves the making of choices between alternative courses of action. Decision making is an integral part of the *other* functions of management—that is, in order to plan, it is necessary to make decisions; in order to organize, it is necessary to make decisions, etc. As a practical matter, decision making is really the culmination of the work of the manager at key points in the planning and control cycle.

C.   The work of management is done most effectively in an organizational structure that is decentralized. Decentralization means the delegation of decision-making authority, by moving the decision-making point to the lowest managerial level possible.

D.   The organization chart is designed to show the levels of responsibility and formal channels of communication in an organization. Basically, a manager may occupy either a line position or a staff position as depicted on the organization chart.

1.   Line positions are those positions which are directly related to the basic objectives of the organization.

2.   Staff positions are those positions which provide service, assistance, and specialized support to the line positions. In this sense, accounting is a staff position; however, authority is delegated to the accounting department by top management to prescribe accounting and reporting procedures which line units must follow.

3.   The controller is the manager of the accounting department. He or she advises top management and heavily influences the decision making process through the providing and interpreting of data.

E.   Organizations can be divided into three basic groups: 1) profit-oriented business enterprises, 2) service-oriented agencies and associations, such as the Red Cross, and 3) service-oriented agencies, such as the Department of Defense, which are created and controlled by governmental bodies. All these organizations share five basic similarities:

1.   Each has an objective toward which it is working.

2.   Each has a set of strategies designed to assist it in achieving its basic objective.

3.   Each has a manager or managers who plan, organize, direct, and control its activities, and who make numerous decisions.

4.   Each has an organizational structure which shows responsibility relationships between managers, and which shows line and staff relationships.

5.   Each has an insatiable need for information to assist in the execution of its strategies.

F.   Information is the "motor" which makes management go. Information comes to management from many directions, one of which is from the accounting department. The information provided by accounting is largely quantitative in nature and is provided to help management do three things:

1.   To plan effectively
2.   To direct operations
3.   To solve problems

G.   There are at least eight major differences between financial and managerial accounting:

1.   Managerial accounting focuses on providing data for internal uses.

2.   Managerial accounting places more emphasis on the future than does financial accounting.

3.   Managerial accounting is not governed by generally accepted accounting principles.

4. Managerial accounting places more emphasis on relevance and flexibility of data than does financial accounting

5. Managerial accounting places less emphasis on precision than does financial accounting and more emphasis on nonmonetary data.

6. Managerial accounting emphasizes the segments of an organization, rather than just looking at the organization as a whole.

7. Managerial accounting draws heavily from other disciplines.

8. Managerial accounting data are optional, whereas most financial accounting data are required.

As these differences suggest, managerial accounting is less structured and less mechanical than is financial accounting. Thus, in order to master the concepts involved in managerial accounting, you will need to devote the bulk of your time to understanding *logic* rather than *mechanical procedure.*

H. The role of managerial accounting is expanding rapidly, due to the operation of many forces on the organization and on its managers.

1. These forces include increased business competition, a severe cost-price squeeze, and rapidly developing technology.

2. For the most part, these forces have intensified the manager's need for information beyond that which is contained in the traditional balance sheet and income statement.

REVIEW AND SELF TEST
Questions and Exercises

True or False

For each of the following statements, enter a T or an F in the blank to indicate whether the statement is true or false.

_____ 1. Managerial accounting is equally as concerned with providing information to stockholders as it is with providing information to managers.

_____ 2. An organization consists of buildings, equipment, and other physical assets dedicated to a common purpose.

_____ 3. The steps to be followed in implementing an organization's objectives are set down through strategic planning.

_____ 4. Strategic planning is sometimes referred to as setting policy.

_____ 5. "Controlling" refers primarily to setting maximum limits on spending in an organization.

_____ 6. The plans of management are expressed in quantitative form as budgets.

_____ 7. In practice, the planning, organizing, and controlling functions of management are kept separate from the decision-making function.

_____ 8. A performance report is a device for obtaining feedback for the manager.

_____ 9. Staff departments in an organization generally have direct authority over line departments.

_____ 10. Profit-oriented organizations and service-oriented organizations share many basic similarities.

_____ 11. The information needs of management are all supplied through the accounting system.

_____ 12. Managerial accounting focuses more on the segments of an organization than on the organization as a whole.

Multiple Choice

Choose the best answer or response by placing the identifying letter in the space provided.

_____ 1. The work of management: a) consists only of strategic planning; b) is clearly explained by the organization chart; c) follows a well-defined cycle; d) responses *a, b,* and *c* are all correct; e) none of these.

_____ 2. Staff positions: a) are not shown on the organization chart; b) are superior in authority to line positions; c) are equal in authority to line positions; d) none of these.

_____ 3. Organizations: a) share only one basic similarity—the need for information; b) share similarities only with other organizations that have like objectives; c) are divided into three basic groups; d) responses _b_ and _c_ are both correct; e) none of these.

_____ 4. The controller: a) has delegated authority over line departments; b) occupies a line position; c) has little influence in the decision-making process; d) none of these.

_____ 5. Managerial accounting: a) is governed by generally accepted accounting principles; b) places more emphasis on precision of data than does financial accounting; c) draws heavily from other disciplines; d) is geared primarily to the past rather than to the future; e) none of these.

_____ 6. Financial and managerial accounting are similar in that: a) both are mandatory; b) both rely on the same accounting information system; c) both focus on providing data for internal uses; d) none of these.

_____ 7. In a decentralized organization, decisions are made: a) only by top management; b) only by managers occupying staff positions; c) at the lowest managerial level possible in the organization; d) none of these.

_____ 8. In large part, "control" in an organization is achieved through: a) decentralization of decision-making authority; b) obtaining feedback on how well the organization is moving toward its objectives; c) preparing an organization chart which shows both line and staff functions; d) none of these.

Complete the Statements

Fill in the necessary words to complete the following statements.

1. An _____ can be defined as a group of people working together for some common purpose.

2. The implementation of an organization's objectives is known as _____ _____.

3. Essentially, the manager carries out four broad functions in an organization: 1 _____, 2 _____ and _____, 3 _____, and 4 _____ _____.

4. In _____, the manager outlines the steps to be taken in moving the organization toward its objectives.

5. Control, in large part, is a function of obtaining useful _____ on how well the organization is doing.

6. In _____ _____ the manager attempts to make rational choices between alternatives.

7. The work of management can be summarized very nicely in a model known as the _____ and _____ cycle.

8. Responsibility relationships between managers are shown on the _____ _____.

9. A _____ department is one whose activities are directly related to the basic objectives of the organization.

10. Strategic planning in an organization is carried out by persons occupying _____ positions.

11. The accounting department has _____ authority over line departments in accounting matters.

12. The plans of management are often expressed as _____.

13. The manager generally is most interested in _____ of information drawn from accounting records, rather than in the details of transactions.

14. As compared to _____ accounting, _____ accounting places much more emphasis on the future.

15. _____ accounting draws heavily from other disciplines.

16. _____ means the delegation of decision-making authority throughout an organization by allowing managers at various operating levels to make key decisions relating to their area of responsibility.

Chapter 1
Answers to Questions and Exercises

True or False

1.	F	7.	F
2.	F	8.	T
3.	T	9.	F
4.	T	10.	T
5.	F	11.	F
6.	T	12.	T

Multiple Choice

1. c
2. d
3. c
4. a
5. c
6. b
7. c
8. b

Complete the Statements

1. organization
2. strategic planning
3. planning, organizing, directing, controlling, decision making
4. planning
5. feedback
6. decision making
7. planning, control
8. organization chart
9. line
10. line
11. delegated
12. budgets
13. summaries
14. financial, managerial
15. Managerial
16. Decentralization

Chapter 2

Cost Terms, Concepts, and Classifications

Chapter Study Suggestions

This chapter introduces general cost terms which will be used throughout the remainder of the book. The chapter also gives a broad outline of the flow of costs in a manufacturing company. (Cost flow is treated in more depth in Chapter 3.) As you read the chapter, note each new term that is introduced and be sure you understand its meaning. Pay particular attention to the concepts of product cost, variable cost, fixed cost, direct cost, indirect cost, and differential cost.

Exhibit 2-3 presents the *schedule of cost of goods manufactured*. The format of this schedule should be put to memory, as well as the material in Exhibits 2-5 and 2-6. Learning the material in these exhibits will help you for Chapter 3 and also lay a foundation for many chapters which follow.

CHAPTER HIGHLIGHTS AND STUDY GUIDE

A.   Manufacturing costs are those costs involved in the manufacture of units of product. Manufacturing costs can be subdivided into three basic elements: direct materials, direct labor, and manufacturing overhead.

1.   Direct materials include those materials which become an integral part of a finished product, and which can be conveniently traced into it.

a. An example of direct materials would be the steel used in manufacturing a file cabinet.

b. Small materials items, such as glue, would be treated as indirect materials and added to manufacturing overhead.

2.   Direct labor consists of those labor costs which are physically traceable to the creation of products in a "hands on" sense.

a. An example of direct labor cost would be the workers on an assembly line in a manufacturing plant.

b. Other labor costs, such as supervisors and janitors, are treated as indirect labor and added to manufacturing overhead.

c. Direct materials and direct labor together are known as prime cost.

3.   Manufacturing overhead consists of all costs of manufacturing except direct materials and direct labor.

a. Synonymous terms for manufacturing overhead are: factory overhead, overhead, factory burden, indirect manufacturing costs, and manufacturing expense.

b. Direct labor and manufacturing overhead together are known as conversion cost.

B.   Nonmanufacturing costs are those costs involved with selling and administrative activities.

1.   Selling costs include all costs associated with the marketing of finished products, including commissions, depreciation of delivery equipment, depreciation of finished goods warehouses, and advertising.

2.   Administrative costs include all costs associated with the general administration of an organization, including secretarial salaries, depreciation of general administrative facilities and equipment, and executive compensation.

C.   The costs of an organization can also be classified as being either product costs or period costs.

1.   Product costs and manufacturing costs are synonymous terms. Thus, product costs include direct materials, direct labor, and manufacturing overhead.

2.   Period costs and nonmanufacturing costs are synonymous terms. Thus, period costs include selling costs and administrative costs.

D.   The income statements and balance sheets prepared by manufacturing firms differ in important respects from those prepared by merchandising firms.

1.   The income statement of a manufacturing firm contains an element termed "cost of goods manufactured." You should study Exhibit 2-3 in the text very carefully; it shows how the cost of goods manufactured is computed.

2.   The balance sheet of a manufacturing firm contains three inventory accounts: Raw Materials, Work in Process, and Finished Goods. By contrast, the balance sheet of a merchandising firm contains only one inventory account—Merchandise Inventory.

a. Raw Materials consists of materials on hand which will be used in the manufacture of units of product.

b. Work in Process consists of units of product only partially completed at the end of a period.

c. Finished Goods consists of units of product which are completed and ready for sale to customers.

E.   Manufacturing costs (direct materials, direct labor, and overhead) are also known as *inventoriable* costs.

1.   The term inventoriable costs arises since direct materials, direct labor, and overhead go into Work in Process and Finished Goods, which are *inventory* accounts. Therefore, direct materials, direct labor, and overhead can end up on the balance sheet as part of these inventory accounts (as assets) if goods are either not completed or not sold at the end of a period.

2.   You should study Exhibit 2-5 in the text with great care. It shows the conceptual flow of manufacturing costs through inventory accounts and the way these costs become an expense (cost of goods sold) on the income statement. *This is a key exhibit for Chapter 2.*

3. We can summarize manufacturing and non-manufacturing cost terms as follows:

Synonymous Cost Terms	*Costs Involved*
Manufacturing costs} Product costs Inventoriable costs)	Direct materials, direct labor, and manufacturing overhead
Nonmanufacturing costs} Period costs)	Selling and administrative expenses

F. Labor costs can be broken down into five main categories: direct labor, indirect labor, idle time, overtime premium, and labor fringe benefits

1. Direct labor has already been discussed. As mentioned earlier, it consists of those factory labor costs which can be physically traced to the creation of products in a "hands on" sense.

2. Indirect labor consists of those factory labor costs which are supportive or supervisory in nature. These would include the labor costs of supervisors, superintendents, custodians, maintenance persons, and others whose services are essential to factory operations, but who do not work directly on the product.

3. Idle time represents the costs of direct labor-workers who are unable to perform their assignments due to material shortages, power failures, and the like. Idle time is treated as part of manufacturing overhead.

4. Overtime premium consists of any amount paid above an employee's base hourly rate.

a. For example, if the base rate is $6 per hour and the employee is paid time-and-a-half for overtime, then the overtime premium would be $3 per hour (*not* $9 per hour).

b. Overtime premium is not charged to specific jobs, but rather is included as part of manufacturing overhead.

5. Labor fringe benefits include employment related costs paid by the employer, such as insurance programs, retirement plans, etc.

a. Many firms include *all* such costs as part of manufacturing overhead.

b. Other firms include only the labor fringe benefits relating to indirect labor as part of manufacturing overhead and treat those benefits relating to direct labor as added direct labor costs.

G. For planning and control purposes, costs are classified as variable and fixed, direct and indirect, and controllable and noncontrollable.

1. Variable costs are those costs which vary, in total, in direct proportion to changes in the volume or level of activity.

a. Variable costs include, for example, direct materials, direct labor, commissions to salespersons, and cost of goods sold.

2. Fixed costs are those costs which remain constant in total amount regardless of changes in the level of activity.

a. Fixed costs include, for example, depreciation, supervisory salaries, and rent.

3. The terms direct cost and indirect cost have no meaning unless one first identifies some object or segment to which the costs are to be related.

a. A direct cost is a cost which can be obviously and physically traced to the object or segment under consideration. For example, if the object under consideration is a unit of product, then the materials and labor involved in its manufacture would both be direct costs.

b. An indirect cost is a cost which must be allocated in order to be assigned to the object or segment under consideration. For example, if the object under consideration is a unit of product, then the manufacturing overhead involved in its manufacture would be an indirect cost.

4. A cost is considered to be controllable at a particular level of management if that level has power to authorize the cost. If a manager has no power to authorize a particular cost, then the cost is not considered to be controllable by that manager.

H. The difference in costs between alternatives is known as differential cost. Differential costs include both cost increases and cost decreases.

1. Cost increases are also known as incremental costs.

2. Cost decreases are also known as decremental costs.

3. Differential costs can be either variable or fixed.

I. An opportunity cost is the potential benefit that is lost or sacrificed when the choice of one course of action requires the giving up of an alternative course of action.

1. Every alternative facing a manager has opportunity costs attached to it.

2. Opportunity costs are not recorded on the books of an organization. They simply represent those benefits which are lost through rejecting some course of action.

J. A sunk cost is a cost which has already been incurred and which cannot be changed by any decision made now or in the future. Sunk costs are never differential costs in decision making.

REVIEW AND SELF TEST
Questions and Exercises

True or False

For each of the following statements, enter a T or an F in the blank to indicate whether the statement is true or false.

_____ 1. A manufacturing firm is more complex than most other types of organizations.

_____ 2. Raw materials consist of basic natural resources, such as iron ore.

_____ 3. A supervisor's salary would be considered direct labor if the supervisor works directly in the factory.

_____ 4. Direct labor combined with direct materials is known as prime cost.

_____ 5. Manufacturing overhead combined with direct materials is known as conversion cost.

_____ 6. Nonmanufacturing costs consist of selling costs and administrative costs.

_____ 7. All selling and administrative costs are period costs.

_____ 8. The terms product cost and manufacturing cost are synonymous.

_____ 9. The cost of goods manufactured is deducted from sales in order to derive gross profit in a manufacturing firm.

_____ 10. Part of a cost such as factory depreciation can end up on the balance sheet as an asset if goods are uncompleted or unsold at the end of a period.

_____ 11. Inventoriable costs and product costs are synonymous terms.

_____ 12. Overtime premium should be charged to the specific jobs worked on during overtime periods.

_____ 13. A variable cost will change in total in proportion to changes in the level of activity.

_____ 14. A fixed cost is constant per unit of product.

_____ 15. Manufacturing overhead is an indirect cost with respect to units of product.

_____ 16. The terms differential cost and incremental cost are used interchangeably, although technically differential cost is a broader concept.

_____ 17. Sunk costs can be either variable or fixed.

_____ 18. Property taxes and insurance on a factory building are examples of manufacturing overhead.

Multiple Choice

Choose the best answer or response by placing the identifying letter in the space provided.

_____ 1. Opportunity costs: a) are usually recorded on the books of an organization; b) represent potential benefits which are lost or sacrificed; c) are rarely present in decision situations; d) responses *a, b,* and *c* are all correct.

_____ 2. Which of the following costs would *not* be a period cost? a) indirect materials; b) advertising; c) administrative salaries; d) all of the above are period costs.

_____ 3. The term used to describe goods moving out of work in process into finished goods is: a) cost of goods sold; b) raw materials; c) period cost; d) cost of goods manufactured; e) none of these.

_____ 4. A machinist earns $10 per hour. During a given week he works 40 hours, of which he is idle 5 hours. For the week: a) $400 cost should be charged to direct labor; b) $50 cost should be charged to overtime premium; c) $50 cost should be charged to overhead; d) $425 cost should be charged to direct labor, and $25 cost should be charged to overhead.

_____ 5. "Manufacturing cost" is synonymous with all of the following terms except: a) product cost; b) inventoriable cost; c) period cost; d) all of the above are synonymous terms.

_____ 6. If the activity level drops by 25 percent, one would expect the variable costs: a) to increase per unit of product; b) to drop in total by 25 percent; c) to remain constant in total; d) to decrease per unit of product.

_____ 7. Which of the following items appears as one element in the computation of cost of goods sold in a manufacturing company? a) direct materials; b) work in process; c) cost of goods manufactured; d) manufacturing overhead.

_____ 8. All of the following would be product costs except: a) indirect materials; b) advertising; c) rent on factory space; d) idle time; e) all of the above would be product costs.

Complete the Statements

Fill in the necessary words to complete the following statements.

1. The term "product costs" is synonymous with the terms _____ costs and _____ costs.

2. The opening finished goods inventory, plus the _____, less the ending finished goods inventory, equals the cost of goods sold in a manufacturing company.

3. Selling costs and administrative costs are also known as _____ costs.

4. From a cost behavior point of view, costs can be classified as being either _____ or _____

5. Direct labor and manufacturing overhead added together are called _____ cost.

6. Cotter keys and other small items of materials used in auto manufacture would probably be classified as _____ _____, and added to manufacturing overhead.

7. _____ costs remain constant in total as the activity level fluctuates.

8. A sunk cost can never be a _____ cost in decision making.

9. Goods only partially completed at the end of a period are placed on the balance sheet as _____ _____ _____ inventory.

10. In terms of cost behavior, sales commissions would be classified as a _____ cost.

Exercises

2-1. Sally Anderson worked 47 hours last week. She was idle 3 hours and spent the remaining 44 hours working directly on the manufacture of finished products. Sally is paid $8 per hour and time-and-a-half for work in excess of 40 hours per week. Allocate her week's wages between direct labor cost and manufacturing overhead.

Direct labor (   ) .... $
Manufacturing overhead:
    _____ (   ) .... $
    _____ (   ) .... _____
Total earnings .... $_____

2-2.   Classify each of the following costs as being either period costs or product costs. If a cost is a period cost, indicate whether it would be part of selling cost or part of administrative cost; if it is a product cost, indicate whether it would be direct or indirect to units of product.

| | | Period Cost | | Product Cost | |
		Selling	Admin.	Direct	Indirect
-	Example: Rent on a sales office	X			
-	Example: Direct materials			X	
a.	Sales commissions				
b.	Rent on a factory building				
c.	Secretarial salaries				
d.	Assembly line workers				
e.	Product advertising				
f.	Cherries in a cannery				
g.	Top management salaries				
h.	Lubricants for machines				
i.	Freight out				
j.	Overtime premium				
k.	Entertainment costs				
l.	Executive training program				
m.	Factory supervisory salaries				

2-3.   From the following data, prepare a schedule of cost of goods manufactured.

Lubricants for machines	$ 4,500
Rent, factory building	16,000
Direct labor	90,000
Indirect materials	2,000
Sales commissions	24,600
Factory utilities	5,800
Insurance, factory	2,000
Purchases of raw materials	120,000
Finished goods, beginning	26,000
Finished goods, ending	31,000
Work in process, beginning	16,000
Work in process, ending	11,500
Administrative expenses, general	72,000
Raw materials, beginning	15,000
Raw materials, ending	5,000

2-4.   Harry has decided to produce and sell surfboards in his spare time. He has a garage which was constructed at a cost of $4,000 several years ago, and which will be used for production purposes. The garage will be depreciated over a 20-year life. Harry has determined that each surfboard will require $30 in wood. He will hire students to do most of the work and pay them $35 for each surfboard completed. He will rent tools needed at a cost of $200 per month. Harry has drawn money out of savings to provide the capital needed to get the operation going. The savings were earning interest at 6 percent annually. An ad agency will handle advertising at a cost of $100 per month. Harry will hire students to sell the surfboards and pay a commission of $20 per board.

Required:

From the foregoing information, identify all the examples you can of the following types of costs (a single item may be identified as more than one type of cost):

Variable cost: _____

_____

Fixed cost: _____

_____

Selling or administrative cost: _____

_____

Product cost: _____

_____

Manufacturing overhead cost: _____

_____

Sunk cost: _____

_____

Opportunity cost: _____

_____

Differential cost (between the alternatives of producing or not producing surfboards): _____

_____

_____

Chapter 2
Answers to Questions and Exercises

True or False

1.	T	7.	T	13.	T
2.	F	8.	T	14.	F
3.	F	9.	F	15.	T
4.	T	10.	T	16.	T
5.	F	11.	T	17.	T
6.	T	12.	F	18.	T

Multiple Choice

1. b
2. a
3. d
4. c
5. c
6. b
7. c
8. b

Complete the Statements

1.	manufacturing, inventoriable	6.	indirect material
2.	cost of goods manufactured	7.	Fixed
3.	period	8.	differential
4.	variable, fixed	9.	work in process
5.	conversion	10.	variable

Exercises

2-1. Direct labor: (44 hours x $8) $352
  Manufacturing overhead:
    Idle time (3 hours x $8) $24
    Overtime premium (7 hours x $4)   28   52
  Total Earnings $404

2-2.

	Period Cost		Product Cost	
	Selling	Admin.	Direct	Indirect
a.	X			
b.				X
c.		X		
d.			X	
e.	X			
f.			X	
g.		X		
h.				X
i.	X			
j.				X
k.	X			
l.		X		
m.				X

2-3. Direct materials:

Raw materials inventory, beginning	$ 15,000	
Add: Purchases of raw materials	120,000	
Raw materials available for use	135,000	
Deduct: Raw materials inventory, ending	5,000	
Raw materials used in production		$130,000
Direct labor		90,000
Manufacturing overhead:		
Lubricants for machines	$ 4,500	
Rent, factory building	16,000	
Indirect materials	2,000	
Factory utilities	5,800	
Insurance, factory	2,000	30,300
Total manufacturing costs		250,300
Add: Work in process, beginning		16,000
		266,300
Deduct: Work in process, ending		11,500
Cost of Goods Manufactured		$254,800

2-4. Variable cost: wood, $30; labor, $35; commission, $20

Fixed cost: garage depreciation, $200; tool rent, $200; advertising, $100.

Selling or administrative cost: advertising, $100; commission, $20.

Product cost: garage depreciation, $200; wood, $30; labor, $35; tool rent, $200.

Manufacturing overhead cost: garage depreciation, $200; tool rent, $200.

Sunk cost: garage depreciation, $200 (the garage has already been purchased and therefore represents a sunk cost).

Opportunity cost: interest on the savings withdrawn.

Differential cost: all costs except the garage depreciation, since all costs except the depreciation could be avoided by not producing surfboards.

Systems Design: Job-Order Costing

Chapter Study Suggestions

This chapter expands on the concepts introduced in Chapter 2 by showing how costs are accumulated in manufacturing organizations for purposes of computing unit costs. The costing method illustrated in the chapter is known as *job-order costing*. Pay particular attention to the section early in the chapter titled "Application of Manufacturing Overhead." *Overhead application is a key concept in the chapter.* Exhibit 3-4 provides a bird's eye view of the overall flow of cost and documents in a job-order cost system.

Exhibits 3-5, 3-6, and 3-7 show how direct materials, direct labor, and overhead costs are added to units of product. Study these exhibits with particular care—the concepts they contain will show up often in the homework material. Exhibits 3-8 and 3-9 summarize the concepts and flows of costs up to that point. Notice from Exhibit 3-9 that the Schedule of Cost of Goods Manufactured has been expanded from that given in Chapter 2. *This schedule should be committed to memory.* Study and then *restudy* the section titled "Problems of Overhead Application," paying particular attention to how the under- and overapplied overhead figures are computed.

CHAPTER HIGHLIGHTS AND STUDY GUIDE

A.   Unit cost data are needed by managers for a variety of purposes.

1. First, unit costs are needed in order to cost inventories on financial statements.

2. Second, unit costs are needed for decision-making purposes. One of the most significant uses of unit cost data is in the setting of selling prices for products.

B.   There are two basic costing systems in use: process costing and job-order costing. These two systems have emerged in response to variations in how the manufacturing process can be carried out.

1. Process costing is employed in those situations where manufacturing involves a single product, such as bricks, that is produced for long periods at a time.

2. Job-order costing is used in those manufacturing situations where many different products or separate jobs are being produced each period. Examples would include special order printing and furniture manufacturing.

3. Regardless of whether one is dealing with process costing or job-order costing, the problem of determining unit costs involves a need for averaging of some type. The essential difference between the two costing methods is the way this averaging is carried out.

C.   Before production can begin, raw materials must be acquired. Upon purchase, materials are placed in the Raw Materials inventory account, which is an asset.

1. Materials are placed into production by means of the Materials Requisition Form. The journal entry is:

Work in Process   XXXX
    Raw Materials   XXXX

2. When materials are placed into production, they are recorded on a job cost sheet, which summarizes all production costs going into a particular job. This is illustrated in Exhibit 3-5 in the text.

3. If a portion of the materials requisitioned are indirect materials (nails, glue, etc.), then the costs of these materials are added to the manufacturing overhead account. The journal entry is:

Work in Process (direct materials)   XXX
Manufacturing Overhead
    (indirect materials)   XXX
    Raw Materials   XXX

D.   Labor costs are accumulated by means of time tickets or time sheets. The time tickets are then analyzed to determine the amount of time spent on various jobs and/or assignments.

1. That labor time spent working directly on specific jobs is termed direct labor. That labor time spent working on supportive tasks (maintenance, janitorial) is termed indirect labor. The entry to record labor costs is:

Work in Process (direct labor)   XXXX
Manufacturing Overhead
    (indirect labor)   XXXX
    Salaries and Wages Payable   XXXX

2. Direct labor costs are recorded on individual job cost sheets at the same time they are recorded in the formal accounts. This is illustrated in Exhibit 3-6 in the text.

E.   As explained in Chapter 2, manufacturing overhead is an *indirect* cost and therefore must be allocated in order to be assigned to units of product. This allocation is carried out through the *predetermined overhead rate.*

1. The predetermined overhead rate is computed *before* a year begins and is based entirely on estimated data. The formula is:

$$\frac{\text{Estimated overhead costs}}{\substack{\text{Estimated base (direct} \\ \text{labor hours, etc.)}}} = \substack{\text{Predetermined} \\ \text{overhead rate}}$$

2. In assigning overhead cost to units of product, the predetermined overhead rate is multiplied by the number of direct labor hours worked on a particular job and the amount of cost entered on the individual job cost sheet. The entry is:

Work in Process   XXXX
    Manufacturing Overhead   XXXX

Turn to Exhibit 3-7 in the text to see how overhead costs flow through the accounts and onto the job cost sheets.

3. The assigning of overhead to jobs is known as the application or absorption of overhead.

4. Notice from Exhibit 3-7 that the application of overhead to production and the incurrence of actual overhead costs represents two separate and distinct processes.

a. When incurred, actual overhead costs are *not* charged to work in process. Notice from the exhibit that they are entered into the manufacturing overhead account (see entries 3-6 in the exhibit).

b. The application of overhead comes later (see entry 7 in the exhibit), when the labor time on various jobs has been accumulated.

F.   After direct materials, direct labor, and overhead costs have been added to jobs and the jobs are completed, they are transferred from Work in Process to Finished Goods to await sale.

1. The entry to record completed jobs is:

Finished Goods   XXXX
    Work in Process   XXXX

2. When completed jobs are later sold, the entry is:

Cost of Goods Sold   XXXX
    Finished Goods   XXXX

3. Exhibits 3-8 and 3-9 are key exhibits in Chapter 3 since they summarize much of the material in the chapter. Study these exhibits with care. Notice particularly that the schedule of cost of goods manufactured in Exhibit 3-9 has been expanded somewhat from the format given in Chapter 2. *The format of this schedule should be put to memory.*

G.   Generally there will be a difference between the amount of overhead cost *applied* to Work in Process and the amount of *actual* overhead cost for a period. This can be seen from the Manufacturing Overhead account in Exhibit 3-8, where there is a $5,000 difference between applied and actual overhead cost.

1. If more overhead cost is applied to Work in Process than has actually been incurred, then a situation of *overapplied* overhead exists.

2. If less overhead cost is applied to work in process than has actually been incurred, then a situation of *underapplied* overhead exists.

3. The formula for computing under- or over-applied overhead is:

Actual overhead costs .... $XXXX
Less overhead costs applied to
  work in process:
    Actual direct labor hours X
    predetermined overhead
    rate   XXXX
Under- or overapplied
  overhead .... $ XXX

4. At the end of a period, under- or overapplied overhead usually is either closed out to Cost of Goods Sold or allocated between Work in Process, Finished Goods, and Cost of Goods Sold.

a. Closing any balance out to Cost of Goods Sold is simpler, since only one account is involved. The entry would be:

Cost of Goods Sold   XXXX
    Manufacturing Overhead   XXXX

This entry assumes that overhead was *underapplied*. The entry would be the reverse if overhead was *overapplied*.

b. Allocating any under- or over-applied overhead is more complex, but it is also more accurate from a costing point of view. The allocation is based on the ending balances in the Work in Process, Finished Goods, and Cost of Goods Sold accounts. Assuming that overhead is *underapplied*, the entry would be:

Work in Process   XXXX
Finished Goods   XXXX
Cost of Goods Sold   XXXX
    Manufacturing Overhead   XXXX

H.   In large companies, multiple overhead rates are often used rather than a single, "plant wide" rate. Overhead rates are set in various departments according to that base which most equitably allocates overhead to the various jobs.

1. As a unit of product moves along the production line, overhead is applied in each separate department where a predetermined overhead rate exists.

2. The total of all of these different overhead applications represents the total overhead cost of the job.

REVIEW AND SELF TEST
Questions and Exercises

True or False

For each of the following statements, enter a T or an F in the blank to indicate whether the statement is true or false.

_____ 1. Product costs are historical figures and therefore are of very little use to the manager.

_____ 2. A company producing furniture would probably use a job-order cost system.

_____ 3. Process costing systems are used in those situations where output is basically homogeneous.

_____ 4. Both job-order and process costing systems utilize averaging concepts in computing unit costs.

_____ 5. Most factory overhead costs are direct costs and therefore can be easily identified with specific jobs.

_____ 6. The predetermined overhead rate is computed using estimates of cost and activity.

_____ 7. The predetermined overhead rate is generally computed on a monthly basis rather than on an annual basis to increase the accuracy of unit costs.

_____ 8. The cost of indirect materials used in production is added to the Manufacturing Overhead account rather than added directly to Work in Process.

_____ 9. The job cost sheet is used to accumulate the costs chargeable to a particular job.

_____ 10. Actual manufacturing overhead costs are charged directly to the Work in Process account as the costs are incurred.

_____ 11. Selling and administrative expenses should be added to the Manufacturing Overhead account.

_____ 12. If more overhead is applied to Work in Process than is actually incurred, then overhead will be overapplied.

_____ 13. All of the raw materials purchased during a period are included in the cost of goods manufactured figure.

_____ 14. Very large firms will often have multiple overhead rates.

_____ 15. A debit balance in the Manufacturing Overhead account at the end of a period would mean that overhead was underapplied for the period.

_____ 16. Any balance in the Work in Process account at the end of a period should be closed to Cost of Goods Sold.

_____ 17. On the Schedule of Cost of Goods Manufactured, any underapplied overhead should be deducted from the actual overhead costs in order to determine the amount of overhead cost applied to Work in Process.

_____ 18. Once production is completed, the job cost sheet can be discarded.

_____ 19. Allocating any under- or overapplied overhead cost between Work in Process, Finished Goods, and Cost of Goods Sold is a more accurate costing approach than closing the entire under- or overapplied amount to Cost of Goods Sold.

_____ 20. Under- or overapplied overhead is computed by deducting actual overhead costs from the amount of overhead cost applied to Work in Process.

Multiple Choice

Choose the best answer or response by placing the identifying letter in the space provided.

_____ 1. Beaver Company bases its predetermined overhead rate on direct labor hours. Its estimates of cost and activity for 19x5 were: overhead, $50,000; direct labor hours, 10,000. During 19x5, Job #410 required 600 direct labor hours. Actual overhead costs for 19x5 totaled $55,000. The amount of overhead charged to Job #410 on the job cost sheet would have been: a) $3,300; b) $120; c) $3,000; d) $8,000; e) none of these.

_____ 2. In a job-order cost system, the basic document for accumulating costs by individual job is: a) the materials requisition form; b) the job cost sheet; c) the Work in Process control account; d) the labor time ticket; e) none of these.

_____ 3. The most common treatment of under- or overapplied overhead is to close it out to: a) Work in Process; b) Retained Earnings; c) Cost of Goods Sold; d) Finished Goods; e) none of these.

_____ 4. Apple Company bases its predetermined overhead rates on machine hours. Its estimates for 19x2 were: overhead, $60,000; machine hours, 40,000. Actual operating data for 19x2 were: overhead, $65,100; machine hours, 42,000. Under- or overapplied overhead for the year would be: a) underapplied, $2,100; b) overapplied, $3,000; c) underapplied, $3,000; d) overapplied. $5,100; e) none of these.

_____ 5. The Work in Process account is a control account supported by detailed cost information contained in: a) the Finished Goods inventory account; b) the Cost of Goods Sold account; c) the job cost sheets of uncompleted jobs; d) the Manufacturing Overhead account; e) none of these.

_____ 6. When a company has a highly automated manufacturing plant, what is probably the most appropriate basis for applying manufacturing overhead cost to jobs: a) direct labor-hours; b) direct labor cost; c) machine hours; d) cost of material used; e) none of these.

_____ 7. On January 1, Hessler Company's Work in Process account had a balance of $18,000. During the year, raw materials costing $40,000 were purchased, and raw materials costing $35,000 were placed into production. Factory labor cost for the year totaled $70,000, of which $60,000 was direct labor. The predetermined overhead rate for the year was set at 150 percent of direct labor cost. Actual overhead costs for the year totaled $92,000. Jobs costing $190,000 to manufacture were completed during the year. On December 31, the balance in the Work in Process inventory account was: a) $13,000; b) $18,000; c) $15,000; d) none of these.

_____ 8. On the schedule of cost of goods manufactured, the final cost of goods manufactured figure: a) represents the amount of cost charged to Work in Process during the period; b) represents the amount transferred from Work in Process to Finished Goods during the period; c) represents the amount of cost placed into production during the period; d) none of these.

_____ 9. If overhead is overapplied for a period, it means that: a) the predetermined overhead rate used to apply overhead cost to Work in Process was too low; b) the company incurred more overhead cost than it charged to Work in Process; c) too much cost has been assigned to units of product; d) none of these.

_____ 10. Marvel Company's Manufacturing Overhead account showed a $10,000 underapplied overhead balance on December 31. Other accounts showed the following balances on that date:

Raw Materials	$ 50,000
Work in Process	40,000
Finished Goods	60,000
Cost of Goods Sold	100,000

If the company allocates the underapplied overhead, the amount allocated to Work in Process would be: a) $2,000; b) $4,000; c) $1,600; d) none of these.

Complete the Statements

Fill in the necessary words to complete the following statements.

1.   A company doing special order printing would very likely use _____ _____ _____ rather than process costing.

2.   Raw materials are drawn from the storeroom on presentation of a_____.

3.   The predetermined overhead rate is computed by dividing estimated _____ _____ by estimated _____ _____ hours or some other activity base.

4.   The_____is used to summarize all of the costs chargeable to a particular job.

5.   Applied manufacturing overhead cost should be debited to the_____. inventory account, and credited to the _____ _____ account.

6.   The process of assigning overhead cost to jobs is known as the _____ or _____ of overhead.

7.   If the amount of overhead cost applied to Work in Process is less than the actual overhead costs of a period, then overhead is _____

8.   The most accurate way to dispose of under- or overapplied overhead is to allocate it between _____, _____, and _____.

9.   Rather than have a single overhead rate, large companies often have_____

10.   A debit balance in the Manufacturing Overhead account indicates that overhead was_____, and a credit balance indicates that overhead was _____

11.   Only_____materials cost and_____labor cost are charged to Work in Process;_____materials cost and_____labor cost are charged to manufacturing overhead.

12.   Labor costs are charged to various jobs by means of a document known as a_____, which shows an hour-by-hour summary of an employee's work.

13.   Manufacturing overhead is an _____ cost to units of product, and thus must be allocated in order to be assigned to jobs.

14. Actual overhead costs incurred during a period are charged to the _____ _____ account, rather than charged to Work in Process.

15. An overhead rate established before a period begins is known as a _____ _____ rate.

Exercises

3-1. Bartle Company uses a job-order cost system. Estimated cost and activity data for 19x5 were: manufacturing overhead, $150,000; direct labor hours, 100,000. At the end of 19x5, cost records revealed that actual overhead costs of $160,000 had been incurred and that 105,000 direct labor hours had been worked.

    a.   The predetermined overhead rate for 19x5 would be .... $_____.

    b.   Manufacturing overhead cost applied to work in process for 19x5 would be .... $_____.

    c.   The amount of underapplied or overapplied overhead cost for 19x5 would be .... (underapplied/overapplied) $_____.

3-2. The following selected account balances are taken from the books of Pardoe Company as of June 1, 19x6, the start of the current year:

Cash		Work in Process		Accounts Payable			
12,000		40,000			75,000		

Accounts Receivable		Finished Goods		Salaries and Wages Payable			
48,000		100,000			12,000		

Prepaid Insurance		Accumulated Depreciation		Sales			
8,000			120,000				

Raw Materials		Manufacturing Overhead		Cost of Goods Sold			
30,000							

The following data relate to the activities of Pardoe Company for the fiscal year ending May 31, 19x7:

1. Raw materials purchased on account, $150,000.
2. Raw materials issued to production, $145,000 (all direct materials).
3. Advertising cost incurred for the year, $50,000.
4. Utilities cost incurred for the factory, $35,000.
5. Salaries and wages costs incurred: direct labor, $250,000 (30,000 hours); indirect labor, $75,000; selling and administrative, $140,000.
6. Depreciation recorded for the year, $20,000, of which 75 percent related to the factory and 25 percent related to selling and administrative functions.
7. Other factory overhead costs incurred for the year, $30,000 (credit accounts payable).
8. Other selling and administrative expenses incurred for the year, $25,000 (credit accounts payable).
9. The prepaid insurance relates to factory operations. One-half of the amount expired during the current year.
10. The company applies overhead cost to production on a basis of direct labor hours, at $5.50 per hour.
11. Goods completed (cost of goods manufactured) for the year totaled $550,000.
12. Goods which had a manufactured cost of $540,000 were sold on account for $800,000.
13. Collections on account from customers during the year totaled $790,000.
14. Cash disbursed during the year: on accounts payable, $300,000; for salaries and wages, $460,000.

Required:

1. Post the entries above directly into Pardoe Company's T-accounts. Key your entries with the numbers 1–14 above.
2. Compute the ending balance in each T-account.
3. Is overhead underapplied or overapplied for the year? _____ Close the balance into Cost of Goods Sold. (Key the entry as #15.)
4. Prepare an income statement for the year.

PARDOE COMPANY
Income Statement
For the Year Ended May 31, 19x7

_____

_____

_____

_____

_____

_____

_____

_____

_____

_____

_____

_____

_____

3-3. From the following data, compute the amount of raw materials used in production during the year:

Direct labor cost	$240,000
Raw materials inventory, 12/31/x5	15,000
Indirect labor cost	90,000
Raw materials inventory, 1/1/x5	10,000
Work in process inventory, 12/31/x5	75,000
Work in process inventory, 1/1/x5	60,000
Purchases of raw materials	145,000

_____

_____

_____

_____

_____

_____

_____

Chapter 3
Answers to Questions and Exercises

True or False

1.	F	8.	T	15.	T
2.	T	9.	T	16.	F
3.	T	10.	F	17.	T
4.	T	11.	F	18.	F
5.	F	12.	T	19.	T
6.	T	13.	F	20.	T
7.	F	14.	T		

Multiple Choice

1.	c	6.	c
2.	b	7.	a
3.	c	8.	b
4.	a	9.	c
5.	c	10.	a

Complete the Statements

1. job-order costing
2. materials requisition form
3. manufacturing overhead, direct labor
4. job cost sheet
5. Work in Process, Manufacturing Overhead
6. application, absorption
7. underapplied
8. Work in Process, Finished Goods, Cost of Goods Sold
9. multiple overhead rates
10. underapplied, overapplied
11. direct, direct, indirect, indirect
12. time ticket
13. indirect
14. Manufacturing Overhead
15. predetermined overhead

Exercises

3-1. a. $\frac{\$150,000}{100,000} = \$1.50/\text{direct labor hour}$

b.   105,000 direct labor hours × $1.50 = $157,500 applied

c.
Actual overhead cost	$160,000
Applied overhead cost	157,500
Underapplied overhead cost	$ 2,500

3-2. The answers to parts 1 and 2 are on the following page.

    3.   Overhead is overapplied.

    4.

PARDOE COMPANY
Income Statement
For the Year Ended May 31, 19x7

Sales		$800,000
Less cost of goods sold		534,000
Gross margin		266,000
Less operating expenses:		
Advertising expense	$ 50,000	
Salaries expense	140,000	
Depreciation expense	5,000	
Other expenses	25,000	220,000
Net Income		$ 46,000

3-3.

Raw materials inventory, 1/1/x5	$ 10,000
Add purchases of raw materials	145,000
Total	155,000
Deduct raw materials inventory, 12/31/x5	15,000
Raw Materials Used in Production	$140,000

(Exercise 3-2) 1. and 2.

Cash	
12,000	760,000(14)
(13)790,000	
------	------
42,000	

Work in Process	
40,000	550,000(11)
(2)145,000	
(5)250,000	
(10)165,000	
------	------
50,000	

Accounts Payable	
(14)300,000	75,000
	150,000 (1)
	50,000 (3)
	35,000 (4)
	30,000 (7)
	25,000 (8)
------	------
	65,000

Advertising Expense
(3) 50,000

Accounts Receivable	
48,000	790,000(13)
(12a)800,000	
------	------
58,000	

Finished Goods	
100,000	540,000(12b)
(11)550,000	
------	------
110,000	

Salaries and Wages Payable	
(14)460,000	12,000
	465,000 (5)
------	------
	17,000

Salaries Expense
(5)140,000

Prepaid Insurance	
8,000	4,000 (9)
------	------
4,000	

Accumulated Depreciation	
	120,000
	20,000 (6)
------	------
	140,000

Sales	
	800,000(12a)

Depreciation Expense
(6)   5,000

Raw Materials	
30,000	145,000 (2)
(1)150,000	
------	------
35,000	

Manufacturing Overhead	
(4) 35,000	165,000(10)
(5) 75,000	
(6) 15,000	
(7) 30,000	
(9) 4,000	
------	------
(15) 6,000	6,000

Cost of Goods Sold	
(12b)540,000	6.000 (15)

Other Selling and Administrative Expense
(8) 25,000

Systems Design: Process Costing

Chapter Study Suggestions

The chapter is divided into five main parts. The first part is a comparison of job-order and process costing. Exhibit 4-1, which outlines the diffrences between the two costing methods, is the key item in this part. The second part deals with journal entries under a process costing system. As you study these entries, note that they are essentially the same as in job-order costing. The third part of the chapter deals with a concept known as *equivalent units of production*. This part will require special effort in order to grasp the concept of equivalent units. Pay particular attention to the computations in Exhibits 4-5 and 4-6.

The last two parts of the chapter deal with the preparation of a production report. The production report is the single most important concept in the chapter. Thus, you will need to focus most of your time and effort on learning how it is constructed. Detailed examples are provided in Exhibits 4-10 and 4-11. Study these exhibits until you are thoroughly acquainted with each step involved in the preparation of a production report.

CHAPTER HIGHLIGHTS AND STUDY GUIDE

A.   Process costing is used in those industries which produce basically homogeneous products such as bricks, flour, and cement. The method is also employed in assembly-type operations, as well as in utilities producing gas, water, and electricity.

B.   Process costing is similar to job-order costing in three ways.

1. The same basic purposes exist in both systems, which are: (a) to assign material, labor, and overhead costs to products; (b) to provide a mechanism for computing unit costs; and (c) to provide data essential for planning, control, and decision making.

2. Both systems maintain and use the same basic manufacturing accounts, including Manufacturing Overhead, Raw Materials, Work in Process, and Finished Goods.

3. Cost flows through the manufacturing accounts in (2) move in basically the same way in both systems.

C.   Process costing differs from job-order costing in four ways.

1. A single product is produced on a continuous basis, and each unit is identical.

2. Costs are accumulated by department, rather than by job.

3. The department production report (rather than the job cost sheet) is the key document showing the accumulation and disposition of cost.

4. Unit costs are computed by department (rather than by job). This computation is made on the department production report.

D.   A processing department is any location in the factory where work is performed on a product and where materials, labor, and overhead costs are added to it.

1. All processing departments have two essential features. First, the activity performed in the department is performed uniformly on all units passing through it. And second, the output of the department is homogeneous.

2. Processing departments can be organized in either a sequential or a parallel pattern. A sequential pattern is where all units go through all departments. A parallel pattern is where not all units go through all departments. Some units may be going through one department while other units are going through other departments, in a parallel fashion.

E.   Cost accumulation is simpler in a process costing system than in a job-order costing system. The reason is that costs only need to be identified with a few processing departments rather than with hundreds (or even thousands) of individual jobs.

F.   Exhibit 4-4 provides a T-account model of cost flows in a process costing system. Key points relating to the flow of these costs follow:

1. A separate Work in Process account is maintained for each processing department. With this separate account, materials, labor, and overhead costs can be entered directly into *any* processing department—not just the first.

2. Assuming a company has two processing departments, A and B, the entry to record materials cost would be:

Work in Process—Department A	XX	
Work in Process—Department B	XX	
Raw Materials		XXXX

3. Since it is not necessary to identify costs with specific jobs, a time clock is generally adequate for accumulating labor costs and allocating them to the proper department. The entry to record labor costs would be:

Work in Process—Department A	XX	
Work in Process—Department B	XX	
Salaries and Wages Payable		XXXX

4. There are two ways of handling overhead costs in a process costing system.

a. The simplest approach is to charge products with the actual overhead costs of the period. (Under this approach, no predetermined overhead rates are computed.) However, this approach works well only if overhead costs are incurred uniformly over a period and if production is stable.

b. If overhead costs are not incurred uniformly or if production is not stable, then predetermined overhead rates must be used to allocate overhead costs to products, the same as in Chapter 3. Each department will have its own predetermined overhead rate. The entry to record the application of overhead cost would be:

Work in Process—Department A	XX	
Work in Process—Department B	XX	
Manufacturing Overhead		XXXX

5. When partially completed units are transferred from one department to another, the entry is:

Work in Process—Department B	XXX	
Work in Process—Department A		XXX

6. When work has been completed in all processing departments, the entry to transfer the completed units into Finished Goods is:

Finished Goods	XXX	
Work in Process—Department B		XXX

7. Finally, when a customer's order is filled and units are sold, the cost of the units is transferred into Cost of Goods Sold, the same as in Chapter 3:

Cost of Goods Sold	XXX	
Finished Goods		XXX

G. Once costs have been accumulated, a department's output must be determined so that unit costs can be computed. A department's output is always stated in terms of equivalent units of production.

1. Equivalent units can be defined as the number of units which would have been produced during a period if all of a department's efforts had resulted in completed units of product.

2. Equivalent units can be computed either by the weighted-averaged method or by the FIFO method.

a. The formula for computing equivalent units by the weighted-average method is:

Units completed and transferred out	XXX
Add: Equivalent units in the ending inventory	XXX
Equivalent units of production	XXX

Under the weighted-average method, units in the *beginning* Work in Process inventory are not used in computing the equivalent units figure. The reason is that these units are treated as if they were started and completed during the current period.

b. The formula for computing equivalent units by the FIFO method is:

Units completed and transferred out	XXX
Add: Equivalent units in the ending inventory	XXX
Total completed units	XXX
Deduct: Equivalent units in the beginning inventory	(XXX)
Equivalent units of production	XXX

3. Since separate unit costs are computed for both materials cost and conversion cost, an equivallent units figure must be computed for each of these cost items.

H. The purpose of the production report is to summarize for the manager all of the activity that takes place in a department's Work in Process account for a period. This activity includes the units which flow through the Work in Process account as well as the costs which flow through it. A production report has three parts:

1. A quantity schedule, which shows the flow of units through a department.

2. A computation of unit costs.

3. A reconciliation of all cost flows into and out of a department during a period.

I. The quantity schedule, which shows the flow of units through a department, is prepared in the same way regardless of whether the weighted-average or the FIFO method is being used to cost units of product.

1. The quantity schedule is self-balancing in that it shows the number of units to be accounted for in a department, and it also shows how those units have been accounted for. The format is:

Units to be accounted for:	
Units in process, beginning	XXX
Units started into production	XXX
Total units to account for	XXX
Units accounted for as follows:	
Units transferred out*	XXX
Units in process, ending	XXX
Total units accounted for	XXX

*Transferred to the next department or to Finished Goods.

2. The quantity schedule deals with whole units, not with equivalent units, although the stage of completion is always shown parenthetically.

J.   The second step in a production report is to compute unit costs. A computation of unit costs under the weighted-average method is shown in Exhibit 4-10, and a computation under the FIFO method is shown in Exhibit 4-11. Note that in the case of the weighted-average method, costs in the beginning Work in Process inventory are added in with current period costs in computing the unit costs for the period.

K.   The final step in a production report is to prepare a reconciliation of all costs for the period. This reconciliation consists of two parts—one part showing the costs which must be accounted for and and the other part showing how these costs are accounted for.

1. Costs which must be accounted for consist of (a) costs in the beginning Work in Process inventory and (b) costs which have been added by the department during the period.

2. Costs are accounted for as being either (a) transferred out during the period or (b) assigned to the ending Work in Process inventory.

a. In transferring out costs under the FIFO method, the units in the beginning Work in Process inventory must be kept separate from the units started and completed during the current period. An example of a completed production report showing this procedure under the FIFO method is provided in Exhibit 4-11. *Study this exhibit with great care, since the material it (and Exhibit 4-10) contains represents the heart of the chapter.*

b. In transferring out costs under the weighted-average method, no distinction is made between units in the beginning Work in Process inventory and units started and completed during the period. This procedure is shown in Exhibit 4-10.

L.   In comparing the weighted-average and FIFO methods, three points can be noted:

1. In most situations, the two methods will produce unit costs which are nearly the same. Any difference is likely to be traceable to raw material prices.

2. From a standpoint of cost control, the FIFO method is superior to the weighted-average method.

3. Although the FIFO method is more complex to apply than is the weighted-average method, this complexity is not a significant factor due to the advent of the computer.

REVIEW AND SELF TEST
Questions and Exercises

True or False

For each of the following statements, enter a T or an F in the blank to indicate whether the statement is true or false.

_____ 1. A utility such as the water company would typically use a process costing system.

_____ 2. Under process costing it is important to identify the materials, labor, and overhead costs associated with a particular customer's order, the same as with job order costing.

_____ 3. If processing departments are arranged in a parallel manner, all units will go through all departments.

_____ 4. In a process costing system, the production report takes the place of the job cost sheet.

_____ 5. Costing is more difficult in a process costing system than it is in a job-order costing system.

_____ 6. Process and job-order costing are similar in that costs are accumulated (and unit costs are computed) for each separate customer order.

_____ 7. In a process costing system, a Work in Process account is maintained for each department.

_____ 8. It is important to identify labor costs with each customer order in a process costing system.

_____ 9. In some situations, it is possible to charge products with actual overhead costs, rather than applied overhead costs, in a process costing system.

_____ 10. Since costs are accumulated by department, there is no need for a Finished Goods inventory account in a process costing system.

_____ 11. In a process costing system, costs incurred in one department remain there rather than being transferred on to the next department.

_____ 12. If the opening Work in Process inventory contains 500 units that are 60 percent complete, then the inventory contains 300 equivalent units.

_____ 13. Under the FIFO method, costs in the opening Work in Process inventory are kept separate from current period costs.

_____ 14. The purpose of the quantity schedule is to show the equivalent units for the period.

_____ 15. Under the FIFO method, units in the opening Work in Process inventory are treated as if they were started and completed during the current period.

_____ 16. Under the FIFO method, units are transferred out in two separate blocks—one block consisting of the units in the opening inventory, and the other block consisting of the units started and completed during the period.

_____ 17. The weighted-average and FIFO methods will typically produce widely different unit costs.

_____ 18. From a standpoint of cost control, the weighted-average method is superior to the FIFO method.

Multiple Choice

Choose the best answer or response by placing the identifying letter in the space provided.

_____ 1. Apple Company started 4,800 units into process during 19x1. Five hundred units were in the opening inventory and 300 units were in the ending inventory. How many units were completed and transferred out during the period? a) 5,000; b) 4,600; c) 5,300; d) 5,100; e) none of these.

_____ 2. During 19x5 Eager Company started 8,000 units into production. The company had 2,000 units in process on January 1 of that year, which were 60 percent complete, and 3,000 units in process on December 31 which were 50 percent complete. 7,000 units were completed and transferred to the next department during the year. Using the FIFO method, the equivalent units for the year would be: a) 8,300; b) 7,700; c) 7,300; d) 6,700; e) none of these.

_____ 3. Refer to the data in question 2 above. Using the weighted average method, the equivalent units for the year would be: a) 8,200; b) 8,500; c) 9,200; d) 9,500; e) none of these.

_____ 4. Costs in the opening Work in Process inventory are added in with costs of the current period when making unit cost calculations by: a) the FIFO cost method; b) the weighted average cost method; c) the quantity schedule method; d) none of these.

_____ 5. Under the weighted average cost method: a) completed units are transferred out in two separate blocks; b) units in the ending inventory are not considered in making equivalent units computations; c) units in the opening inventory are treated as if they were started and completed during the current period.

_____ 6. If all units do not go through all processing departments, then the departments are probably arranged in a: a) sequential pattern; b) linear pattern; c) homogeneous pattern; d) parallel pattern; e) none of these.

Complete the Statements

Fill in the necessary words to complete the following statements.

1. Processing departments might be organized in either a _____ processing pattern or a _____ processing pattern.

2. Rather than using job cost sheets, in a process costing system a document known as a _____ _____ is prepared for each department.

3. In a process costing system, costs are accumulated by _____ rather than by job.

4. A separate _____ _____ _____ account is maintained for each department in a process costing system.

5. A department's output is measured in terms of _____ _____ of production.

6. Under the _____ _____ method, units in the beginning Work in Process inventory are treated as if they were started and completed during the current period.

7. The purpose of the _____ _____ is to account for the physical flow of units through a department during a period.

8. Under the _____ method, units in the beginning Work in Process inventory are kept separate from units started and completed during the current period.

9. From a standpoint of cost control, the _____ method is superior to the _____ _____ method.

10. On a production report, labor and overhead costs are often added together and called _____ costs.

Exercises

4-1. Diebold Company has a process costing system. Data relating to activities in the Mixing Department for March 19x6 follow:

	Units	Percent Completed Materials	Percent Completed Conversion
Work in process, March 1	5,000	100	60
Units started into production	80,000		
Work in process, March 31	2,000	100	50

Prepare a quantity schedule for the Mixing Department for the month:

Units

Units to be accounted for:

Units accounted for as follows:

4.2 Sinclair Company uses a process costing system. Complete the production report below for the company's Cooking Department by showing how the $277,300 in cost charged to the department for the period is to be accounted for. The company uses the FIFO cost method.

Production Report, Cooking Department

Quantity schedule				*Units*
Units to be accounted for:				
Units in process, beginning (all materials; 25% labor and overhead)				8,000
Units started into production				62,000
Total units to account for..				70,000
Units accounted for as follows:				
Units transferred out				65,000
Units in process, ending (all materials; 80% labor and overhead)				5,000
Total units accounted for				70,000

Computation of unit costs	*Materials*	*Labor*	*Overhead*	*Total*
Cost added by the department (a)	$93,000	$134,000	$33,500	$260,500
Computation of equivalent units:				
Units transferred out	65,000	65,000	65,000	
Add: Equivalent units, ending				
Work in Process	5,000	4,000	4,000	
Total completed units	70,000	69,000	69,000	
Deduct: Equivalent units, beginning				
Work in Process	8,000	2,000	2,000	
Equivalent units of production (b)	62,000	67,000	67,000	
Unit cost (a) ÷ (b)	$1.50	$2.00	$0.50	$4.00

Cost reconciliation	Units	Costs
Cost to be accounted for:		
Work in process, beginning	8,000	$ 16,800
Added by the department during the month	62,000	260,500
Total cost to be accounted for	70,000	$277,300

Cost accounted for as follows:
1) Transferred to the next department
    Units from the beginning inventory:
        Cost in the beginning inventory .... $
        Cost to complete these units:
           Labor cost (   ) ....
           Overhead cost (   ) ....
             Total cost....................................
        Units started and completed during
          the month (   )
             Total cost transferred .... $
2) Work in process, ending
    Materials cost (   ) .... $
    Labor cost (   ) ....
    Overhead cost (   ) ....
        Total cost in Work in Process, ending............
        Total cost accounted for $277,300

4-3. Minden Company has a process costing system and uses the weighted-average method. Complete the production report below for the company's Mixing Department by showing how the $470,000 in cost charged to the department for the period is to be accounted for.

Production Report, Mixing Department

Quantity schedule	Units
Units to be accounted for:	
Units in process, beginning (all materials; 20% labor and overhead)	5,000
Units started into production..	75,000
Total units to account for	80,000
Units accounted for as follows:	
Units transferred out..	72,000
Units in process, ending (all materials; 75% labor and overhead)....................	8,000
Total units accounted for	80,000

Computation of unit costs

	Materials	Labor	Overhead	Total
Work in process, beginning	$ 4,500	$ 3,000	$ 2,000	$ 9,500
Cost added by the department....................	75,500	231,000	154,000	460,500
Total cost (a)................................	$80,000	$234,000	$156,000	$470,000
Equivalent units:				
Units transferred out	72,000	72,000	72,000	
Add: Equivalent units, ending				
Work in proces.........................	8,000	6,000	6,000	
Equivalent units of production (b)............	80,000	80,000	80,000	
Unit cost (a) ÷ (b)	$1.00	$3.00	$2.00	$6.00

Cost reconciliation

	Units	Costs
Cost to be accounted for:		
Work in process, beginning.............................	5,000	$ 9,500
Added by the department during the month	75,000	460,500
Total cost to be accounted for	80,000	$470,000
Cost accounted for as follows:		
Transferred out ( ).....................		$
Work in process, ending		
Materials ( )......................		$
Labor ( )...........................		
Overhead ( )......................		
Total cost of work in process, ending		
Total cost accounted for		$470,000

Chapter 4
Answers to Questions and Exercises

True or False

1.	T	7.	T	13.	T
2.	F	8.	F	14.	F
3.	F	9.	T	15.	F
4.	T	10.	F	16.	T
5.	F	11.	F	17.	F
6.	F	12.	T	18.	F

Multiple Choice

1. a
2. c
3. b
4. b
5. c
6. d

Complete the Statements

1.	sequential, parallel	6.	weighted-average
2.	production report	7.	quantity schedule
3.	department	8.	FIFO
4.	Work in Process	9.	FIFO, weighted-average
5.	equivalent units	10.	conversion

Exercises

4-1.

	Units
Units to be accounted for:	
Units in process, March 1 (all materials; 60% conversion cost)	5,000
Units started into production	80,000
Total units to be accounted for	85,000
Units accounted for as follows:	
Transferred out during the month	83,000
Units in process, March 31 (all materials; 50% conversion cost)	2,000
Total units accounted for	85,000

4-2.

	Units	Costs
Cost accounted for as follows:		
1) Transferred to the next department....................	65,000	
Units from the beginning inventory:		
Cost in the beginning inventory......................		$ 16,800
Cost to complete these units:		
Labor cost (8,000 × 75% × $2)......................		12,000
Overhead cost (8,000 × 75% × $0.50)		3,000
Total cost		31,800
Units started and completed during the month		
(57,000 × 100% × $4).................................		228,000
Total cost transferred		$259,800
2) Work in process, ending	5,000	
Materials cost (5,000 × 100% × $1.50)		$ 7,500
Labor cost (5,000 × 80% × $2)..........................		8,000
Overhead cost (5,000 × 80% × $0.50)		2,000
Total cost in work in process, ending		17,500
Total cost accounted for	70,000	$277,300

4-3.

	Units	Costs
Cost accounted for as follows:		
Transferred out (72,000 × 100% × $6)	72,000	$432,000
Work in process, ending	8,000	
Materials (8,000 × 100% × $1)		$ 8,000
Labor (8,000 × 75% × $3)		18,000
Overhead (8,000 × 75% × $2)		12,000
Total cost in work in process, ending...................		38,000
Total cost accounted for	80,000	$470,000

Cost Behavior: Analysis and Use

Chapter Study Suggestions

Chapter 5 expands on the discussion of fixed and variable costs which was started in Chapter 2. In addition, the chapter introduces a new cost concept—mixed costs—and shows how mixed costs can be broken down into their basic fixed and variable elements. Focus the bulk of your study time on the section titled, "The Analysis of Mixed Costs," which is found midway through the chapter. Pay particular attention to how a *cost formula* is derived from the data in Exhibits 5-8 and 5-9 and how these cost formulas are used to predict future costs at various activity levels.

Commit to memory the elements of the equation: $Y = a + bX$. Also study carefully how this equation ties in with the "Least Squares" method of cost analysis. When this is completed, you will have the bulk of the chapter under your belt. At the end of the chapter, a new format to the income statement called the "contribution approach" is introduced, which gears the income statement to cost behavior. The format of the contribution income statement is found in Exhibit 5-11. *This format should be put to memory immediately—* you will be using it throughout the rest of the book.

At the end of the chapter, there is a review problem which you should work before attempting any of the homework material.

CHAPTER HIGHLIGHTS AND STUDY GUIDE

A. A variable cost is a cost which varies, in total, in direct proportion to changes in the activity level. Variable costs are constant on a *per unit basis*.

1. Variable costs are shown graphically in Exhibit 5-1. Notice that the relationship between cost and activity is *linear*. This is a key idea which is discussed in more detail a little later.

2. Variable costs vary according to some activity base. The most common activity bases are hours worked, units produced, and units sold. Other activity bases include miles driven by salespersons, the number of beds in a hospital, and the number of letters typed by a secretary.

3. Direct materials and direct labor are both variable costs. Manufacturing overhead consists of both variable and fixed costs.

4. Variable costs may be either true variable or step variable.

    a. A true variable cost is one which varies in direct proportion to changes in activity. Direct materials is an example of such a variable cost.

    b. A step variable cost is one which is obtainable only in fairly large chunks and which increases or decreases only in response to fairly wide changes in the activity level. The labor cost of maintenance persons is such a variable cost.

    c. The behavior patterns of true variable and step variable costs are shown graphically in Exhibit 5-3.

5. The accountant assumes a strictly linear relationship between cost and volume when dealing with variable costs.

    a. Many variable costs actually behave in a curvilinear fashion, such as illustrated in Exhibit 5-4.

    b. Although the accountant recognizes that many costs behave in a curvilinear fashion, he or she concentrates on their behavior within the band of activity known as the relevant range.

    c. Within the relevant range, the relationship between cost and activity is basically linear.

B. A fixed cost is a cost which remains constant in total, regardless of changes in the activity level. When expressed on a per unit basis, fixed costs vary inversely with changes in the activity level. As the activity level rises, fixed costs per unit fall; as the activity level falls, fixed costs per unit rise.

1. Fixed costs are becoming more significant due to automation and trends toward stabilization of employee salaries.

2. Fixed costs can generally be classified into two categories: committed and discretionary.

    a. Committed fixed costs are those costs which relate to the investment in plant, equipment, and the basic organization of a firm.

    b. Discretionary fixed costs arise from annual decisions by management to spend in certain fixed costs areas, such as advertising, research, and management development programs.

    c. There generally is more flexibility in the year-to-year control of discretionary fixed costs than there is in the control of committed fixed costs. Committed fixed costs tend to be very inflexible.

3. The concept of the relevant range also has application in dealing with fixed costs, particularly those of a discretionary nature. This is illustrated in Exhibit 5-6.

C. A mixed cost is a cost which contains both variable and fixed cost elements. Mixed costs are sometimes known as semivariable costs. The behavior pattern of a mixed cost is shown graphically in Exhibit 5-7.

1. Mixed costs are generally made up of manufacturing overhead. Examples of mixed costs include electricity, heat, repairs, and maintenance.

2. The fixed portion of a mixed cost represents the basic, minimum charge for having the service involved ready and available for use. The variable portion represents the charge made for actual consumption of the service.

3. Several methods are available for breaking a mixed cost down into its basic variable and fixed cost elements. These methods include the high-low method, the scattergraph method, and the least squares method.

D. The high-low method requires that costs be observed both at high and at low levels of activity within the relevant range.

1. The difference in cost observed at the two extremes is divided by the change in activity in order to determine the amount of variable cost involved. The formula is:

$$\frac{\text{Change in cost}}{\text{Change in activity}} = \text{Variable rate}$$

2. Once the variable rate has been determined, it can be used to determine the amount of fixed cost involved in the mixed costs:

Total cost observed at the "high" activity
   level .... $XXXX
Less variable portion:
  Variable rate X "high" level of activity   XXX
Fixed portion of the mixed cost .... $ XX

3. The fixed and variable cost elements can be expressed in a *cost formula,* which can be used to predict costs at other levels of activity within the relevant range.

4. In a cost formula, cost represents the *dependent* variable, and activity represents the *independent* variable.

5. The high-low method is the least accurate method of analyzing mixed costs. This is because the high and low points may not be representative of costs throughout the *entire* relevant range. The high and low points simply represent extremes.

E. The scattergraph method plots all observed costs at various activity levels on a graph. A *regression line* is then fitted to the plotted points by visual inspection.

1. The slope of the regression line represents the variable cost rate. The point where the regression line cuts the cost axis represents total fixed cost.

2. The scattergraph method is more accurate than the high-low method, since it considers all observed points in computing a cost formula rather than just the high and low points.

F. The least squares method fits a regression line to scattergraph data by means of statistical analysis. Thus, it is the most accurate method available for analyzing mixed costs.

1. The least squares method is based on two simultaneous linear equations, which can be employed to determine the fixed and variable elements of a mixed cost. The formulas are:

$$\Sigma XY = a\Sigma X + b\Sigma X^2$$
$$\Sigma Y = na + b\Sigma X$$

where: a = fixed cost, b = variable costs, n = number of observations, X = activity measure (hours, etc.), Y = total mixed cost observed.

2. These equations are based on the formula for a straight line, which is:

$$Y = a + bX$$

The elements in this formula (a, b, etc.) represent the same things as the elements in the equations above.

G. If there is more than one basis of variability in a mixed cost, then *multiple regression analysis* must be used to separate the fixed and variable elements.

H. Internally, the manager generally organizes costs on the income statement according to cost behavior in what is known as the *contribution format.*

1. Variable expenses are deducted first to yield the contribution margin. Contribution margin can be defined as the amount remaining from sales after covering variable expenses, which is available to contribute toward covering of fixed costs, and then toward profits.

2. Fixed costs are then deducted from the contribution margin, and the remainder represents the profits of the period.

3. The format of the contribution income statement is given in Exhibit 5-11. This format should be put to memory.

REVIEW AND SELF TEST
Questions and Exercises

True or False

For each of the following statements, enter a T or an F in the blank to indicate whether the statement is true or false.

_____ 1. Variable costs are costs which change, in total, in direct proportion to changes in the activity level.

_____ 2. In cost analysis work, activity is known as the dependent variable.

_____ 3. Within the relevant range, the higher the activity level, the lower the fixed costs will be when expressed on a per unit basis.

_____ 4. Mixed costs are also known as semivariable costs.

_____ 5. Contribution margin and gross margin are synonymous terms.

_____ 6. Contribution margin is the difference between sales and variable expenses.

_____ 7. Discretionary fixed costs arise from annual decisions by management to spend in certain program areas.

_____ 8. Advertising would be an example of a committed fixed cost.

_____ 9. Mixed costs can be defined as costs which contain both manufacturing and nonmanufacturing cost elements.

_____ 10. The accountant assumes a linear relationship between cost and activity within the relevant range, so far as variable costs are concerned.

_____ 11. In order for a cost to be a variable, it must vary with either units produced or units sold.

_____ 12. The relevant range has no significance so far as fixed costs are concerned.

_____ 13. There is a strong trend in industry today toward more fixed costs.

_____ 14. The cost formula produced by the high-low method and the scattergraph method would generally be the same.

_____ 15. A regression line is a line of averages, with the average variable cost per unit represented by the slope of the line.

_____ 16. The contribution approach to the income statement organizes costs according to behavior, rather than according to function.

Multiple Choice

Choose the best answer or response by placing the identifying letter in the space provided.

_____ 1. Sparks Company's cost formula for maintenance is: $Y = \$4,000 + \$3X$, based on machine hours. During a period, 2,000 machine hours were worked. The expected cost for maintenance would be: a) \$12,000; b) \$6,000; c) \$10,000; d) none of these.

_____ 2. The costs associated with a company's basic plant, equipment, and organization are known as: a) committed costs; b) discretionary costs; c) linear costs; d) variable costs; e) none of these.

_____ 3. For 19x5, Barker Company's sales were \$240,000, its fixed costs were \$50,000, and its variable costs were \$2 per unit. During the year, 80,000 units were sold. The contribution margin for 19x5 was: a) \$200,000; b) \$240,000; c) \$30,000; d) \$80,000; e) none of these.

_____ 4. The regression line derived by the least squares equation: a) is curvilinear; b) is the best possible fit of a regression line to the data; c) generally has a downward slope; d) can be represented by the equation $Y = ab + X$; e) none of these.

_____ 5. An example of a discretionary fixed cost would be: a) depreciation on equipment; b) rent on a factory building; c) salaries of top management; d) items *a, b,* and *c* are all discretionary fixed costs; e) none of these.

_____ 6. Fixed costs are most easily (and most safely) dealt with: a) on a per unit basis; b) on a total basis; c) on a contribution margin basis; d) on a manufacturing basis; e) none of these.

Complete the Statements

Fill in the necessary words to complete the following statements.

1.   A variable cost is _____ per unit, but varies _____ _____ in direct proportion to changes in the activity level.

2.   Variable costs can be divided into two classes, true variable costs and _____ variable costs.

3.   The accountant concentrates on the behavior of costs within a narrow band of activity called the _____ _____.

4.   Fixed costs can be divided into two categories, _____ and _____.

5.   In analyzing mixed costs, the _____ method is probably the least accurate of the three methods available.

6.   In analyzing mixed costs, the scattergraph method fits a _____ line to plotted points by visual inspection.

7.   The expression "$5,000 fixed costs, plus $10 per hour" would be called a cost _____

8.   A straight line can be expressed in equation form as _____

9.   The contribution approach gears the income statement to _____ _____

10.   Contribution margin is the difference between _____ and _____ _____

11.   The traditional income statement organizes costs in a _____ format.

Exercises

5-1. Doughby Company has observed its electrical costs as follows over the relevant range of 5,000 to 8,000 machine hours:

6,800 hrs.	$1,770
6,000 hrs.	1,650
5,400 hrs.	1,560
7,900 hrs.	1,935

a. Using the high-low method, what is the variable rate per machine hour? .... $_____

	Cost	Machine Hours
High point observed		
Low point observed	_____	_____
Difference	_____	_____

$$\frac{\text{Change in Cost}}{\text{Change in Activity}} = \text{_____} = \quad /\text{Machine Hour}$$

b. What is the total fixed cost? .... $_____

Total cost at the "high" activity level ....$
Less variable cost element:

_____   .... _____
Fixed cost element ....$ _____

c. Express the cost formula for electrical costs:

_____

_____

_____

_____

_____

_____

5-2. Data on a week's activity in the shipping department of Osan, Inc., are given below:

Day	Units Shipped (X)	Shipping Cost (Y)	XY	X²
Monday	12	$ 580	$ 6,960	144
Tuesday	17	655	11,135	289
Wednesday	10	550	5,500	100
Thursday	7	505	3,535	49
Friday	9	535	4,815	81
Saturday	5	475	2,375	25
	60	$3,300	$34,320	688

a. Using the least squares method, determine the variable rate per unit shipped:

Equation (1): $\Sigma XY = a\Sigma X + b\Sigma X^2$
Equation (2): $\Sigma Y = na + b\Sigma X$

Equation (1) data:
Equation (2) data:

Multiply equation (1) by _____:
Multiply equation (2) by _____: _____
Subtract (2) from (1):
Variable rate

b. Determine the fixed cost per day:

Equation (2) data from above:

Substitute the variable rate for the "b" term in equation (2):

Solve equation (2) for term "a":

c. Express the cost formula for shipping costs in the form $Y = a + bX$:

5-3. During July 19x3, Simple Company (a merchandising firm) sold 500 units of product. The company's income statement for the month follows:

SIMPLE COMPANY
Income Statement
For the Month Ended July 31, 19x3

Sales ($100/unit)		$50,000
Less cost of goods sold ($60/unit)		30,000
Gross margin		20,000
Less operating expenses:		
Commissions ($6/unit)	$3,000	
Salaries	8,000	
Advertising	6,000	
Shipping ($2/unit)	1,000	18,000
Net Income		$ 2,000

Redo the company's income statement for the month, by presenting it in the contribution format:

SIMPLE COMPANY
Income Statement
For the Month Ended July 31, 19x3

_____

_____

_____

_____

_____

_____

_____

_____

_____

_____

_____

_____

Chapter 5
Answers to Questions and Exercises

True or False

1.	T	9.	F
2.	F	10.	T
3.	T	11.	F
4.	T	12.	F
5.	F	13.	T
6.	T	14.	F
7.	T	15.	T
8.	F	16.	T

Multiple Choice

1. c
2. a
3. d
4. b
5. e
6. b

Complete the Statements

1. constant, in total
2. step
3. relevant range
4. committed, discretionary
5. high-low
6. regression
7. formula
8. $Y = a + bX$
9. cost behavior
10. sales, variable expenses
11. functional

Exercises

5-1. a. Variable rate: $.15 per machine hour.

	Cost	Machine Hours
High point observed	$1,935	7,900
Low point observed	1,560	5,400
Difference	$ 375	2,500

$$\frac{\text{Change in cost} \quad \$375}{\text{Change in activity 2,500 hours}} = \$.15 \text{ per machine hour}$$

b. Total fixed cost: $750 per period.

Total cost at the "high" activity level $1,935
Less variable cost element:
  7,900 hours $\times$ $.15 per hour .... <u>1,185</u>
Fixed Cost Element .... <u>$ 750</u>

c. Cost formula for electrical costs: $750 per period, plus $.15 per machine hour.

5-2. a. Equation (1) data: $34,320 = 60a + 688b
     Equation (2) data: $ 3,300 = 6a + 60b

Multiply equation (1) by 1:	$34,320 = 60a + 688b
Multiply equation (2) by 10:	<u>$33,000 = 60a + 600b</u>
Subtract (2) from (1):	$ 1,320 = 88b
Variable rate:	$ 15 = b

b. Equation (2) data from above: $3,300 = 6a + 60b
    Substitute the variable rate for
      the "b" term in equation (2): $3,300 = 6a + 60 ($15)
    Solve equation (2) for term "a": $3,300 = 6a + $900
                                    $2,400 = 6a
                                    $ 400 = a

c. Y = $400 + $15X

5-3.

SIMPLE COMPANY
Income Statement
For the Month Ended July 31, 19x3

Sales		$50,000
Less variable expenses:		
Cost of goods sold ($60/unit)	$30,000	
Commissions ($6/unit)	3,000	
Shipping ($2/unit)	<u>1,000</u>	<u>34,000</u>
Contribution margin		16,000
Less fixed expenses:		
Salaries	8,000	
Advertising	<u>6,000</u>	<u>14,000</u>
Net Income		<u>$ 2,000</u>

Chapter 6

Cost-Volume-Profit Relationships

Chapter Study Suggestions

Chapter 6 can be described as one of the "key" chapters in the book. What you do in many chapters ahead will depend on concepts developed here. In your study, there are several sections in the chapter that should be given particular attention. The first of these is the section early in the chapter titled, "Contribution Margin." Notice the relationship illustrated here between contribution margin and net income and how the latter is affected by the former. The next section to be studied with particular care is the one titled, "Contribution Margin Ratio." The C/M ratio discussed there is used in most of the analytical work in the chapter.

Another section to be given particular attention is the one titled, "Some Applications of CVP Concepts." Much of the homework material is drawn from this section, so be sure you understand the examples given. The section titled, "Break-Even Analysis" is also drawn from heavily in the homework material. *You should commit the break-even formulas given in this section to memory.* Finally, the latter part of the chapter contains a section titled, "The Concept of Sales Mix," which shows the impact of CVP concepts on multiple-product firms. Notice particularly how the break-even point is computed if a company has more than one product line.

In studying the material in the chapter, try especially hard to understand the *logic* behind solutions given. Keep in mind that CVP analysis represents a *way of thinking,* rather than a mechanical set of procedures.

CHAPTER HIGHLIGHTS AND STUDY GUIDE

A. It is very helpful to the manager to think of contribution margin in *per unit* terms, as well as in total amount.

    1. Each unit sold will generate a fixed amount of contribution margin—the difference between the unit's selling price and its variable expenses.

    2. Total contribution margin can be computed by multiplying the contribution margin per unit times the number of units sold.

        a. Contribution margin is first applied to cover the fixed costs.

        b. The break-even point is reached when the contribution margin generated on sales just equals the fixed costs.

        c. Once the break-even point is reached, net income will increase by the unit contribution margin for each additional unit sold.

    3. The concept contained in part 2 *c.* above provides the manager with a very powerful planning tool. It gives him or her the ability to predict what profits will be at various activity levels without the necessity of preparing detailed income statements.

B. The percentage of contribution margin to total sales is known as the contribution margin ratio (C/M ratio) or as the profit/volume ratio (P/V ratio). It shows how contribution margin will be affected by a given dollar change in sales.

    1. The formula for computing the impact on contribution margin of a change in sales is:

$$\begin{array}{l}\text{Dollar increase} \\ \text{or decrease in} \\ \text{sales}\end{array} \times \begin{array}{l}\text{C/M} \\ \text{ratio}\end{array} = \begin{array}{l}\text{Dollar increase} \\ \text{or decrease in} \\ \text{contribution} \\ \text{margin}\end{array}$$

    2. Any increase in contribution margin will be reflected dollar-for-dollar in increased net income, if the fixed costs do not change.

    3. The C/M ratio is often of more use to the manager than the unit contribution margin figure, particularly when a company has multiple product lines.

        a. The reason the C/M ratio is more useful is because it is in ratio form, which makes it easier to compare product lines as to relative profitability.

        b. Those product lines should be concentrated on which have the highest C/M ratio figures.

C. A company often has some latitude in trading off between fixed and variable costs. There is no categorical answer to the question as to whether it is beneficial to make such trade-offs.

    1. A company with low fixed costs and high variable costs (a low C/M ratio) will enjoy greater stability in net income, but will do so at the risk of losing substantial profits if sales trend sharply upward over time.

    2. A company with high fixed costs and low variable costs (a high C/M ratio) will experience wider movements in net income as sales fluctuate up and down, but will reap greater profits if sales trend sharply upward over time.

D. Operating leverage measures the change in net income which will result from a given change in sales volume.

    1. The formula for computing operating leverage is:

$$\frac{\text{Contribution margin}}{\text{Net income}} = \begin{array}{l}\text{Degree of operating} \\ \text{leverage}\end{array}$$

    2. The operating leverage figure is multiplied times the anticipated *percentage* increase in sales, to obtain the *anticipated* percentage increase in net income, e.g., if the degree of operating leverage is 5, and sales are expected to increase by 10 percent, then net income should increase by:

$$5 \times 10\% = 50\%$$

    3. The degree of operating leverage decreases in amount the further a company moves away from its break-even point.

E. There are many applications of CVP concepts in day-to-day decision making in an organization. Study carefully the examples given under the heading "Some Applications of CVP Concepts" in the early part of the chapter.

    1. Notice that each example makes use of either the unit contribution margin figure or the C/M ratio in arriving at an answer. This underscores the importance of these two concepts.

2. Also notice that several of the examples employ a technique known as *incremental analysis*. An incremental analysis is based only on those items of cost or revenue that will *change* as between alternatives.

3. These examples show clearly that the purpose of CVP analysis is to help the manager to find the most profitable combination of variable costs, fixed costs, selling price and sales volume.

a. The effect on the contribution margin is a major consideration in deciding on the most profitable combination of these factors.

b. There is no magic formula that applies to all organizations, in terms of the mix of costs, selling price and sales volume. Each organization must determine that mix which maximizes its profits.

F. The break-even point can be defined either (1) as the point where total sales equal total expenses, variable and fixed, or (2) as the point where total contribution margin equals total fixed expenses.

1. These two definitions show the two ways the break-even point can be computed. For definition (1) above, the break-even formula is:

$$\text{Sales} = \frac{\text{Variable expenses} + \text{Fixed expenses} + \text{Profits}}{}$$

a. A zero figure for "profits" is entered into the formula when the break-even point is being computed.

b. This formula can also be used to compute the activity level at which a *target net profit* figure will be realized. This is done by inserting the target net profit figure into the "profits" part of the formula.

2. For definition (2) above, the break-even formula is:

$$\frac{\text{Total fixed expenses}}{\text{Unit contribution margin}} = \text{Break-even point (in units)}$$

or

$$\frac{\text{Total fixed expenses}}{\text{C/M ratio}} = \text{Break-even point (in dollars)}$$

a. This is known as the "unit contribution method." It actually is just a variation of the equation method given above.

b. These formulas can also be used to compute the activity level at which a target net profit

figure will be realized. This is done by adding the target net profit figure to the "total fixed expenses" figure in the formulas above.

G. Break-even analysis can also be done graphically. Exhibits 6-1 through 6-5 show how the appropriate graphs are prepared.

1. Exhibits 6-1 and 6-2 relate to the conventional cost-volume-profit graph. This is also known as a "break-even chart." *Study carefully how the graph is prepared and how it is interpreted.*

a. This is called a cost-volume-profit graph because it shows more than just a break-even point. It shows the relationships between sales, costs, and volume throughout wide ranges of activity.

2. Exhibit 6-3 shows an alternate format to the cost-volume-profit graph that is preferred by some managers. This format shows the fixed expenses on top of the variable expenses—the reverse of the conventional graph in Exhibit 6-2. It also shows the contribution margin.

3. Exhibits 6-4 and 6-5 relate to the "profit-graph." It is preferred by some managers because it shows how profits change with changes in sales volumes.

H. The margin of safety (M/S) can be defined as the excess of budgeted (or actual) sales over the break-even volume of sales. It states the amount by which sales can drop before losses begin to be incurred in a company.

1. The formula for computing the margin of safety is: Total sales − Break-even sales = Margin of safety.

2. The margin of safety can also be expressed in percentage form, by dividing the margin of safety in dollars by total sales:

$$\frac{\text{Margin of safety in dollars}}{\text{Total sales}} = \text{Margin of safety percentage}$$

I. Commissions to salespersons are often based on the total contribution margin which the salespersons are able to generate, rather than on total sales. This has the beneficial effect of encouraging the salespersons to focus their efforts on selling those products which will maximize total contribution margin, rather than total sales.

J.   Sales mix is defined as the relative proportion of total units sold (or total sales dollars) which is represented by each of a company's several product lines.

1.   When a company has more than one product line, the break-even point must be computed by using the *overall* C/M ratio, considering the mix of products being sold. The formula is:

$$\frac{\text{Total fixed expenses}}{\text{Overall C/M ratio}} = \frac{\text{Company break-}}{\text{even point}}$$

2.   As the mix of products being sold changes, *the overall C/M ratio will also change.* If the shift in mix is toward the less profitable products, then the overall C/M ratio will fall; if the shift is toward the more profitable products, then the overall C/M ratio will rise. The break-even point will change inversely with changes in the overall C/M ratio.

K.   There are five limiting assumptions in cost-volume-profit analysis:

1.   That the behavior of both revenues and expenses is linear throughout the entire relevant range.

2.   That expenses can be accurately divided into variable and fixed categories.

3.   That the sales mix is constant.

4.   That inventories do not change in break-even computations.

5.   That worker productivity and efficiency do not change.

REVIEW AND SELF TEST
Questions and Exercises

True or False

For each of the following statements, enter a T or an F in the blank to indicate whether the statement is true or false.

_____ 1.   If product A has a higher unit contribution margin than product B, then product A will always have a higher C/M ratio than product B.

_____ 2.   The break-even point occurs where the contribution margin is equal to total variable expenses.

_____ 3.   One of the assumptions of break-even analysis is that there is no change in inventories.

_____ 4.   The break-even point can be expressed either in terms of units sold or in terms of total sales dollars.

_____ 5.   If the product mix changes, a break-even point that was valid in the past may no longer be valid.

_____ 6.   As sales exceed the break-even point, a high C/M ratio will result in lower profits than will a low C/M ratio.

_____ 7.   A firm with a high C/M ratio will have greater operating leverage at a given level of sales than will a firm with a low C/M ratio.

_____ 8.   If sales increase by 8 percent, and the degree of operating leverage is 4, then profits can be expected to increase by 12 percent.

_____ 9.   The degree of operating leverage for a given firm remains the same at all levels of sales activity.

_____ 10.   Once the break-even point has been reached, net income will increase by the unit contribution margin for each additional unit sold.

_____ 11.   A shift in sales mix toward less profitable products will cause the overall break-even point to fall.

_____ 12.   An incremental analysis will focus on changes in costs between two alternatives.

_____ 13.   If a company's cost structure shifts toward greater fixed costs, one would expect the company's C/M ratio to fall.

_____ 14.   One of the major conceptual lessons in this chapter is that the effect on the contribution margin is a key consideration in most cost/revenue decisions.

_____ 15.   One way to compute the break-even point is to divide total sales by the C/M ratio.

_____ 16. Basing sales commissions on contribution margin is generally less desirable from the company's standpoint than basing sales commissions on gross sales.

_____ 17. A key assumption in break-even analysis is that the sales mix will not change.

_____ 18. One approach to the cost-volume-profit graph is to place the fixed expenses on top of the variable expenses, so that the contribution margin can be shown.

Multiple Choice

Choose the best answer or response by placing the identifying letter in the space provided.

_____ 1. If sales are $50,000, variable expenses are $30,000, and fixed expenses are $12,000, the contribution margin ratio is: a) 16 percent; b) 60 percent; c) 40 percent; d) 24 percent; e) none of these.

_____ 2. The break-even point in a given situation would be decreased by an increase in: a) the ratio of variable costs to sales; b) the C/M ratio; c) total fixed costs; d) the mix of less profitable products sold; e) none of these.

_____ 3. If the total contribution margin increases and fixed costs do not change, then net income can be expected: a) to increase by an equal amount; b) to decrease by an equal amount; c) to increase by an amount equal to the increase in contribution margin times the C/M ratio; d) none of these.

_____ 4. In multiple product firms, a shift in the sales mix from less profitable products to more profitable products will cause the company's break-even point to: a) increase; b) decrease; c) there will be no change in the break-even point; d) none of these.

_____ 5. The most important use of the cost-volume-profit graph is to show: a) the break-even point; b) the C/M ratio at various levels of sales activity; c) the relationship between volume, costs, and revenues over wide ranges of activity; d) none of these.

_____ 6. As a company moves further from its break-even point, one would expect the degree of operating leverage to: a) decrease; b) increase; c) remain unchanged; d) vary in direct proportion to changes in the activity level; e) none of these.

_____ 7. The following figures are taken from Parker Company's income statement: Net income, $30,000; Fixed costs, $90,000; Sales, $200,000; and C/M ratio,

60 percent. The company's margin of safety in dollars is: a) $150,000; b) $30,000; c) $50,000; d) none of these.

_____ 8. Refer to the data in question 7 above. The margin of safety in percentage form is: a) 60 percent; b) 75 percent; c) 40 percent; d) 25 percent; e) none of these.

Complete the Statements

Fill in the necessary words to complete the following statements.

1. Product X sells for $10 per unit and requires variable expenses of $6.50 per unit. Product Y sells for $8 per unit and requires variable expenses of $2.40 per unit. For Product X, the unit contribution margin is $_____, and the contribution margin ratio is _____ For Product Y, the unit contribution margin is $_____, and the contribution margin ratio is _____

2. Refer to the data in Question 1 above. At a given level of sales, one would expect Product _____ to have the highest degree of operating leverage.

3. Refer again to the data in Question 1 above. Assuming that total fixed costs will be the same to produce and sell either product, Product_____ will have the lowest break-even point.

4. Any increase in contribution margin will be reflected dollar-for-dollar in increased net income, so long as the _____ _____ do not change.

5. The relative proportion of various products represented in a company's total sales is called the _____ _____

6. The cost-volume-profit equation is: Sales = _____ _____ + _____ _____ + _____

7. Some companies feel that the way to maximize overall profits is to base sales commissions on _____ _____ rather than on gross sales.

8. Other things equal, managers should seek out and promote those products which have the highest _____ _____ _____

9. On a CVP graph, the break-even point is where the total revenue line crosses the _____ _____ line.

10. At a given level of sales, the contribution margin divided by the net income yields a figure known as the _ _____ _____

Exercises

6-1. Hardee Company sells a single product. The selling price is $30 per unit and the variable expenses are $18 per unit. The company's most recent income statement is given below:

Sales (4,500 units)	$135,000
Less variable expenses	81,000
Contribution margin	54,000
Less fixed expenses	48,000
Net Income	$ 6,000

a.   Compute the contribution margin per unit .... $_____

b.   Compute the C/M ratio .... _____%

c.   Compute the break-even point in sales dollars .... $_____

d.   Compute the break-even point in units sold .... _____ units

e.   How many units must be sold next year to double the company's profits? ..... _____ units

f.   Compute the company's degree of operating leverage .... _____

g.   Sales for next year (in units) are expected to increase by 5 percent. Using the operating leverage concept, net income should increase by .... _____%

h.   Prove your answer to part *g* by preparing a contribution income statement showing a 5 percent increase in sales.

_____

_____

_____

_____

_____

6-2. From the data below, construct a cost-volume-profit graph like the one in Exhibit 6-2 in the text:

Sales: 15,000 units at $10 each.
Variable expenses: $6 per unit.
Fixed expenses: $40,000 total.

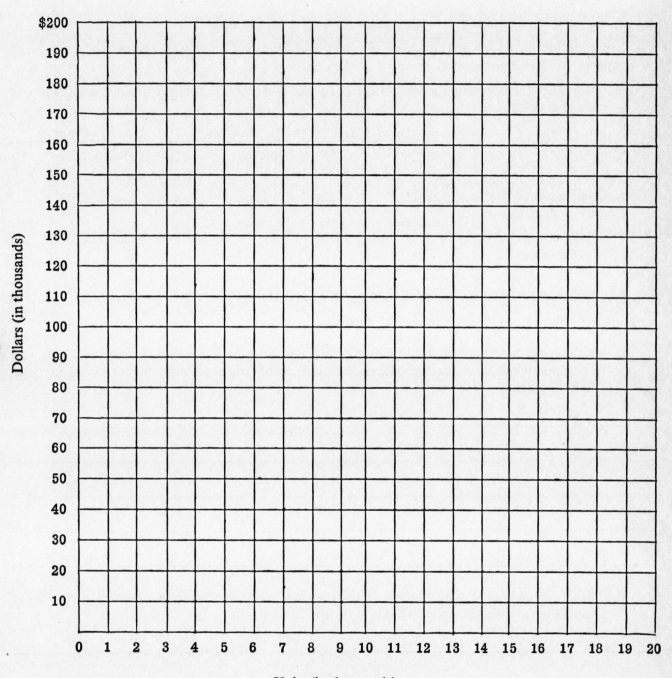

Units (in thousands)

What is the break-even point:

In units? _____

In total sales dollars? _____

6-3. Seaver Company produces and sells two products, X and Y. Cost and revenue data on the products follow:

	Product X	Product Y
Selling price per unit	$10	$12
Variable expenses per unit	6	3
Contribution margin per unit	$ 4	$ 9

In the most recent month, the company sold 400 units of Product X and 600 units of Product Y. Fixed expenses are $5,000 per month.

a.   Complete the following income statement for the most recent month (carry percentages to one decimal point):

	Product X Amount	%	Product Y Amount	%	Total Amount	%
Sales	$		$		$	
Less variable expenses						
Contribution margin	$		$			
Less fixed expenses						
Net income (loss)					$	

b.   Compute the company's overall monthly break-even point in sales dollars ....$_____

c.   If the company continues to sell 1,000 units, in total, each month, but the sales mix shifts so that an equal number of units of each product is being sold, would you expect monthly net income to rise or fall? Explain.

_____

_____

_____

_____

_____

d.   Refer to the data in part c above. If the sales mix shifts as explained, would you expect the company's monthly break-even point to rise or fall? Explain.

_____

_____

_____

_____

_____

Chapter 6
Answers to Questions and Exercises

True or False

1.	F	7.	T	13.	F
2.	F	8.	F	14.	T
3.	T	9.	F	15.	F
4.	T	10.	T	16.	F
5.	T	11.	F	17.	T
6.	F	12.	T	18.	T

Multiple Choice

1. c
2. b
3. a
4. b
5. c
6. a
7. c
8. d

Complete the Statements

1. $3.50, 35%, $5.60, 70%
2. Y
3. Y
4. fixed costs
5. sales mix

6. variable expenses, fixed expenses, profits
7. contribution margin
8. contribution margin ratio
9. total expenses
10. operating leverage

Exercises

6-1. a.

	Unit	
Selling price	$30	100%
Less variable expenses	18	60
Contribution Margin	$12	40%

b. $\dfrac{\text{Contribution Margin } \$12}{\text{Selling Price} \qquad \$30} = 40\% \text{ C/M Ratio}$

c. Sales = Variable Expenses + Fixed Expenses + Profits

$$X = .60X + \$48,000 + \$-0-$$
$$.40X = \$48,000$$
$$X = \$120,000$$

Alternate solution:

$$\frac{\text{Total Fixed Expenses } \$48,000}{\text{C/M Ratio} \qquad\qquad .40} = \$120,000$$

d.   Sales = Variable Expenses + Fixed Expenses + Profits

$30X = $18X + $48,000 + $-0-
$12X = $48,000
    X = 4,000 units

Alternate solution:

$$\frac{\text{Total Fixed Expenses}}{\text{Unit Contribution Margin}} \quad \frac{\$48,000}{\$12} = 4,000 \text{ units}$$

e.   Sales = Variable Expenses + Fixed Expenses + Profits

$30X = $18X + $48,000 + $12,000
$12X = $60,000
    X = 5,000 units

Alternate solution:

$$\frac{\text{Total Fixed Expenses + Target Net Income}}{\text{Unit Contribution Margin}} \quad \frac{\$48,000 + \$12,000}{\$12} = 5,000 \text{ units}$$

f. $$\frac{\text{Contribution Margin}}{\text{Net Income}} \quad \frac{\$54,000}{\$ 6,000} = 9$$

g.   5% × 9 = 45%

h.   New sales volume: 4,500 units × 105% = 4,725 units

Sales (4,725 units)	$141,750
Less variable expenses (4,725 units)	85,050
Contribution margin	56,700
Less fixed expenses	48,000
Net Income	$ 8,700
Present net income	$ 6,000
Expected increase: $6,000 × 45%	2,700
Expected Net Income (as above)	$ 8,700

6-2. The completed CVP graph:

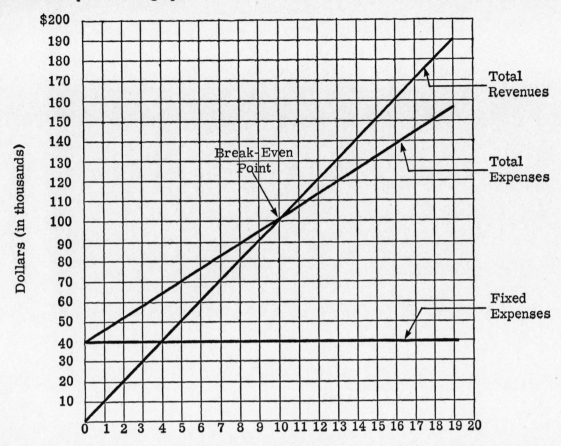

Units (in thousands)

The break-even point in units: 10,000. The break-even point in dollars: $100,000.

6-3. a. The completed income statement:

	Product X		Product Y		Total	
	Amount	*%*	*Amount*	*%*	*Amount*	*%*
Sales	$4,000	100	$7,200	100	$11,200	100.0
Less variable expenses	2,400	60	1,800	25	4,200	37.5
Contribution margin	$1,600	40	$5,400	75	7,000	62.5
Less fixed expenses					5,000	
Net income					$ 2,000	

b. $\dfrac{\text{Fixed Expenses}\quad \$5,000}{\text{Overall C/M Ratio}\quad 62.5\%} = \$8,000$ in sales to break even.

c. Monthly net income will fall. The shift in sales mix will mean that less of Product Y is being sold and more of Product X is being sold. Since Product Y has a higher contribution margin per unit than does Product X, this means that less contribution margin *in total* will be available, and profits will therefore fall.

d. The monthly break-even point will rise. As explained above, the shift in sales mix will be toward the less profitable Product X, which has a C/M ratio of only 40 percent as compared to 75 percent for Product Y. Thus, the company's *average* C/M ratio will fall, and the break-even point will rise since less contribution margin will be available per unit to cover the fixed costs.

Chapter 7

Segmented Reporting, and the
Contribution Approach to Costing

Chapter Study Suggestions

The chapter is divided into two parts. The first part deals with segmented reporting, and the second part deals with the contribution approach to costing. The two parts are related in that internally the manager uses the contribution approach in preparing segmented reports.

Before you start reading the part of the chapter dealing with segmented reporting, study Exhibits 7-1, 7-2, and 7-3. These exhibits illustrate what is meant by the term "segmented reporting." Notice particularly that on a segmented report the total company is divided into smaller parts, so that the manager can look at various pieces of the company, rather than just at the whole. In studying the text material, spend the time necesssary to fully understand the difference between direct and common fixed costs, and the difference between segment margin and contribution margin.

In the second part of the chapter we introduce a new method of costing manufactured goods, called direct costing. This is actually just a variation of the contribution approach to preparing an income statement, with which you are already familiar. We are just extending the contribution approach to *costing manufactured goods* and calling it by a slightly different name. There are four exhibits in this part—Exhibits 7-5 through 7-8. *Study these exhibits with great care;* they hold the key to understanding the material in this part of the chapter. If you can follow these exhibits through step-by-step, then you should have a minimum of difficulty with the homework material.

CHAPTER HIGHLIGHTS AND STUDY GUIDE

A. To operate effectively, the manager needs much more information than that provided by a single income statement. He or she needs information that focuses on the *segments* of his or her organization.

    1. A segment can be defined as any part or activity of an organization about which the manager seeks cost data. Examples of segments would include sales territories, manufacturing divisions, producing departments and/or operations, and groups or lines of products.

    2. Internally, segmented reports are prepared in the contribution format with which you are already familiar.

    3. Exhibit 7-1 contains an illustration of one way that a series of segmented reports can be prepared. Notice that as we go from one segmented report to another in the exhibit, we are looking at smaller and smaller pieces of the company.

    4. By preparing segmented reports such as those illustrated in Exhibit 7-1, the manager may uncover problems that otherwise would have remained hidden from view. For example, some product lines may be unprofitable; some sales territories may have a poor sales mix; other sales territories may be using ineffective promotional strategies, etc. Problems such as these can be highlighted by the use of segmented reports.

B. Two general guidelines are used in allocating costs to the various segments when the contribution approach is used.

    1. First, costs are allocated according to cost behavior patterns; that is, according to whether they are variable or fixed.

    2. Second, costs are allocated according to whether they are *direct* or *indirect (common)* to the various segments.

        a. Only direct costs are charged directly to a segment.

        b. Indirect (common) costs are not charged to the segments; rather, common costs are kept separate from the segments and charged only against the company as a whole.

C. A key concept in the chapter is the distinction between direct and common fixed costs.

    1. From Chapter 2, the guidelines for distinguishing between direct and indirect (common) costs are:

        a. If a cost can be obviously and physically traced to a unit of product or other organizational segment, then it is a direct cost with respect to that segment.

        b. If a cost must be *allocated* in order to be assigned to a unit of product or other organizational segment, then it is an indirect (common) cost with respect to that segment.

    2. The placement of direct and common fixed costs on a segmented income statement is as follows:

	Total	Segment A	Segment B
Sales	$XXXX	$XX	$XX
Less variable expenses.	XXX	X	X
Contribution margin..	XXX	X	X
Less direct fixed expenses	XX	X	X
Segment margin	XX	$ X	$ X
Less common fixed expenses	X		
Net Income	$ X		

    3. Classifications between direct and common fixed costs are not static. As an organization is segmented into smaller and smaller pieces, some costs which were previously direct will become common. This is because there are limits to how finely a cost can be divided.

    4. The segment margin is a highly useful piece of data, showing the manager the long-run profitability of a segment after it has covered all of the costs which can be traced directly to it.

a. The segment margin is used by the manager in decision situations relating to long-run needs and performance, such as capacity changes, long-run pricing policy, and segment return on investment.

b. By contrast, the contribution margin is most useful in those situations involving short-run decisions, such as pricing of special orders and special promotional campaigns.

5. Common costs are not allocated to segments, since such an allocation would destroy the usefulness of the segment margin as a tool for assessing segment performance.

a. In addition, allocating common costs may create a bias for or against a particular segment, since such allocations are always arbitrary in nature.

D. In order to provide the manager with more detailed information, a company may show total sales broken down into several different segment arrangements.

1. For example, a company may choose to break total sales down in two ways: first, according to product lines; and second, according to sales territories without respect to the product lines sold within the territories.

2. An illustration of this type of segmented reporting is given in Exhibit 7-4. Also study Exhibit 7-3 carefully, which shows the degree of segmentation which is possible by this approach to segmented reporting.

3. After segmenting total sales in various ways, such as illustrated in Exhibit 7-4, managers then often further segment each part by dividing it into finer pieces, such as illustrated earlier in the chapter in Exhibit 7-1.

a. All of this segmentation gives the manager the power to look at his/her company from many different directions and at many different levels.

E. Manufacturing firms must have a way of costing units of product so that the manager can prepare a contribution-type income statement for his or her own use internally.

1. This is accomplished through a concept known as *direct costing*. Under direct costing, only the variable manufacturing costs are treated as product costs and added to the cost of a unit of product.

a. Variable manufacturing costs would include only direct materials, direct labor, and the variable portion of manufacturing overhead.

2. Fixed manufacturing costs are treated as *period* costs and charged against the period in which the costs were incurred, the same as are fixed selling and administrative expenses.

a. Advocates of direct costing argue that fixed manufacturing costs relate to the *capacity* to produce rather than to the production of specific units of product in any given year.

b. Thus, fixed manufacturing costs should be charged against the period, and not added to the inventoriable cost of units produced.

3. Essentially, the difference in the way direct costing and absorption costing handle fixed manufacturing overhead costs centers on a matter of timing.

a. Under direct costing, all fixed manufacturing costs are charged to expense immediately as a period cost, as explained.

b. Under absorption costing, all fixed manufacturing costs are added to the cost of products, and then charged to expense slowly, bit-by-bit, as the products are sold.

F. Exhibit 7-6 is a key exhibit illustrating the differences between direct and absorption costing. *Study this exhibit carefully before going on.* Several important generalizations relative to direct versus absorption costing can be drawn from the data in the exhibit.

1. When production and sales (in units) are equal, the same net income will be reported under either direct or absorption costing.

2. When production exceeds sales (in units), greater net income will be reported under absorption costing than under direct costing.

a. The reason is that under absorption costing fixed costs are deferred in inventory. The amount deferred is equal to the excess production times the fixed production cost per unit.

3. When production is less than sales, less net income will be reported under absorption costing than under direct costing.

a. The reason is that under absorption costing fixed costs are released from inventory. The amount released is equal to the excess units sold times the fixed production cost per unit.

4. Over an *extended* time, the net income reported by the two costing methods will tend to be the same. The following format can be used to reconcile the direct and absorption costing net income figures:

Direct costing net income .... $ XX
Add: fixed production costs deferred in
       inventory under absorption
       costing   XX
Deduct: fixed production cost released
          from inventory under absorp-
          tion costing..................   (XX)
Absorption costing net income .... $ XX

G.   Exhibit 7-8 is another key exhibit, showing the effects of changes in production on net income under both direct and absorption costing.

1. Net income under direct costing is not affected by changes in production. Net income is affected only by changes in the number of units sold.

2. Net income under absorption costing tends to be affected by changes in production, increasing as production increases, and vice-versa.

a. This is a major criticism of absorption costing, since an organization can thus increase its reported net income by simply increasing production.

REVIEW AND SELF TEST
Questions and Exercises

True or False

For each of the following statements, enter a T or an F in the blank to indicate whether the statement is true or false.

_____ 1. Common costs should be allocated to product line segments on a basis of sales dollars.

_____ 2. A series of segmented reports focuses on progressively smaller pieces of an organization.

_____ 3. Contribution margin is basically a short-run planning tool and is especially valuable in decisions relating to temporary uses of capacity, special orders, and short-run promotional strategy.

_____ 4. A key idea relating to the contribution approach to costing is that fixed costs are relatively unimportant in most organizations.

_____ 5. The terms "direct cost" and "variable cost" are synonymous.

_____ 6. If a cost must be allocated in order to be charged to a unit of product or other organizational segment, then it is an indirect (common) cost with respect to that segment.

_____ 7. As an organization is broken down into smaller segments, costs that were direct to the larger segments may become common to the smaller segments.

_____ 8. The segment margin is viewed as being the best gauge of the long-run profitability of a segment.

_____ 9. It generally is not possible to segment total sales in more than one way.

_____ 10. Fixed manufacturing overhead costs are treated the same way under both the direct costing and absorption costing methods.

_____ 11. The direct costing method is not acceptable for income tax purposes or for external reporting.

_____ 12. Absorption costing data are generally better suited for cost-volume-profit analysis than direct costing data.

_____ 13. The direct costing method treats fixed manufacturing overhead as a period cost rather than as a product cost.

_____ 14. When sales are constant but the level of production fluctuates, the absorption costing method will produce a more stable net income pattern than will the direct costing method.

_____ 15. When production and sales are equal, the same net income will be reported regardless of whether direct costing or absorption costing is being used.

_____ 16. When production exceeds sales, fixed overhead costs are deferred in inventory under absorption costing.

_____ 17. Under the direct costing method, variable selling and administrative costs are treated as product costs along with direct materials, direct labor, and variable manufacturing overhead.

_____ 18. When sales exceed production, fixed overhead costs are released from inventory under absorption costing.

Multiple Choice

Choose the best answer or response by placing the identifying letter in the space provided.

_____ 1. If a cost cannot be traced directly to certain segments of an organization, it should be: a) allocated to the segments on some meaningful basis, such as sales dollars; b) excluded from the income statement; c) deducted in total as a common cost; d) none of these.

_____ 2. Armco, Inc., produces and sells five product lines. Which of the following costs would typically be a direct fixed cost of one product line: a) advertising costs of the product lines; b) the salary of the company's president; c) depreciation of facilities used jointly to produce several product lines; d) responses a, b, and c are all correct.

_____ 3. The segment margin, as contrasted to the contribution margin, is most useful for: a) making short-run decisions, such as accepting special orders at special prices; b) assessing the long-run performance of a segment; c) determining the best way to allocate common costs among segments; d) responses b and c are both correct; e) none of these.

_____ 4. White Company manufactures a product known as a Zet. The following unit costs are associated with each Zet:

Direct materials	$3
Direct labor	4
Variable overhead	1
Variable selling and administrative expense	2

In addition, fixed manufacturing overhead costs total $100,000 each period. The company normally produces 20,000 Zets each period. The cost of a single Zet under the absorption costing method would be: a) $10; b) $13; c) $15; d) none of the these.

_____ 5. Refer to the data in question 4 above. The cost of a single Zet under the direct costing method would be: a) $8; b) $10; c) $13; d) none of these.

_____ 6. If sales exceed production, one would expect net income under the direct costing method to be: a) the same as net income under the absorption costing method; b) less than net income under the absorption costing method; c) greater than net income under the absorption costing method; d) none of these.

_____ 7. Which of the following costs are treated as period costs by the direct costing method: a) variable and fixed manufacturing overhead; b) fixed manufacturing overhead; c) all manufacturing costs, fixed and variable; d) none of these.

_____ 8. During 19x2, Peck Company produced 10,000 units and sold 9,000 units. Fixed overhead costs total $20,000 annually, and variable overhead costs are $3 per unit. For 19x2, one would expect net income under the absorption costing method to be: a) $2,000 more than net income under the direct costing method; b) $5,000 more than net income under the direct costing method; c) $2,000 less than net income under the direct costing method; d) $5,000 less than net income under the direct costing method.

_____ 9. Which of the following is viewed as being an advantage of the direct costing method: a) direct costing data can be used more easily in cost-volume-profit analysis; b) the profit of a period is not affected by changes in inventories when the direct costing method is used; c) direct costing income figures facilitate relative appraisal of products, territories, classes of customers and other segments of a business; d) responses a, b, and c are all correct; e) none of these.

Complete the Statements

Fill in the necessary words to complete the following statements.

1. In order to uncover problems such as unprofitable product lines and a poor sales mix, the manager needs income statement data that focus on the _____ of his company.

2. Costs that are shared jointly by several segments of an organization are called indirect or _____ costs.

3. The manager should treat as _____ costs of a segment only those costs which would disappear if the segment itself disappeared.

4. The _____ margin is viewed as being the best gauge of the long-run profitability of a segment.

5. One approach to segmented reporting is to break _____ _____ down into several different segment arrangements.

6. Only _____ manufacturing costs are treated as product costs under the direct costing method.

7. If sales exceed production, fixed overhead costs are _____ from inventory under absorption costing.

8.   For external reporting on financial statements, a company is required to cost units of product by the _____ costing method.

9.   Direct costing could more accurately be called _____ or _____ costing.

10.   The inventory carrying value under absorption costing will always be _____ in dollar amount than the inventory carrying value under direct costing.

Exercises

7-1. From the following data, prepare a segmented income statement for the Bylund Company for July 19x8:

	Total	Product X	Product Y
Number of units sold	--	10,000	12,000
Selling price per unit	--	$20.00	$25.00
Variable cost per unit:			
Production	--	9.00	10.00
Selling and administrative	--	3.00	3.75
Fixed costs:			
Production	$155,000		
Selling and administrative	20,000		

Some $50,000 of the fixed production costs relate directly to the production of Product X and $75,000 relate directly to the production of Product Y.

BYLUND COMPANY
Income Statement
For the Month Ended July 31, 19x8

	Total		Product X		Product Y	
	Amount	%	Amount	%	Amount	%
Sales	$_____	__	$_____	__	$_____	__
Less variable expenses:						
Total variable expenses	_____		_____		_____	
Contribution margin						
Less direct fixed expenses	_____		_____		_____	
Product line segment margin	_____		_____		_____	
Less common fixed expenses:						
Total fixed expenses	_____					
Net Income	$_____					

7-2. Selected data relating to the operations of Dole Company for 19x1 are given below:

Units produced	40,000
Units sold	35,000
Fixed costs:	
Manufacturing overhead	$160,000
Selling and administration	140,000
Variable costs per unit:	
Direct materials	7
Direct labor	6
Manufacturing overhead	3
Selling and administration	2

a. Assume that the company uses absorption costing. Compute
the cost to produce one unit of product .... $_____

Determine the value of the ending inventory .... $_____

b. Assume that the company uses direct costing. Compute the
cost to produce one unit of product .... $_____

Determine the value of the ending inventory .... $_____

c. Which method would show the highest net income for 19x1?
(Direct costing/absorption costing) By how much? .... $_____

7-3. The Hodex Company was organized just one month ago. The company manufactures and sells a unique product that has been quickly accepted by consumers. The results of the company's first month of operations are shown below (absorption costing basis):

Sales (10,000 units @ $20)	$200,000
Less cost of goods sold (10,000 units @ $14)	140,000
Gross margin	60,000
Less selling and administrative expenses	45,000
Net Income	$ 15,000

Variable selling and administrative expenses are $2 per unit. The company produced 12,000 units during the month. Variable manufacturing costs total $10 per unit, and fixed manufacturing overhead costs total $48,000 per month.

a. Redo the company's income statement in the contribution format, using direct costing.

_____

_____

_____

_____

_____

_____

_____

_____

_____

_____

_____

_____

_____

_____

_____

b. Reconcile the direct costing and absorption costing net income figures:

Direct costing net income .... $

Absorption costing net income $15,000

Chapter 7
Answers to Questions and Exercises

True or False

1.	F	7.	T	13.	T
2.	T	8.	T	14.	F
3.	T	9.	F	15.	T
4.	F	10.	F	16.	T
5.	F	11.	T	17.	F
6.	T	12.	F	18.	T

Multiple Choice

1.	c	6.	c
2.	a	7.	b
3.	b	8.	a
4.	b	9.	d
5.	a		

Complete the Statements

1.	segments	6.	variable
2.	common	7.	released
3.	direct	8.	absorption
4.	segment	9.	variable, marginal
5.	total sales	10.	greater (higher)

Exercises
7-1.

BYLUND COMPANY
Income Statement
For the Month Ended July 31, 19x8

	Total		Product X		Product Y	
	Amount	*%*	*Amount*	*%*	*Amount*	*%*
Sales	$500,000	100	$200,000	100	$300,000	100
Less variable expenses:						
Production	210,000	42	90,000	·45	120,000	40
Selling and administrative	75,000	15	30,000	15	45,000	15
Total variable expenses	285,000	57	120,000	60	165,000	55
Contribution margin	215,000	43	80,000	40	135,000	45
Less direct fixed expenses	125,000	25	50,000	25	75,000	25
Product line segment margin	90,000	18	$ 30,000	15	$ 60,000	20
Less common fixed expenses:						
Production	30,000					
Selling and administrative	20,000					
Total fixed expenses	50,000					
Net Income	$ 40,000					

7-2. a.

Direct materials	$ 7
Direct labor	6
Variable overhead	3
Fixed overhead ($160,000 ÷ 40,000 units)	4
Total Cost per Unit	$20

Ending Inventory: 5,000 units × $20   = $100,000

b.

Direct materials	$ 7
Direct labor	6
Variable overhead	3
Total Cost per Unit	$16

Ending Inventory: 5,000 units × $16   = $80,000

c.   Absorption costing would show the highest net income, by $20,000. The reason is that the inventory has increased by 5,000 units, and each unit has taken $4 of fixed overhead cost into inventory with it, thus relieving these costs from the income statement.

7-3. a.

Sales (10,000 units @ $20)		$200,000
Less variable expenses:		
Variable cost of goods sold @ $10	$100,000	
Selling and administrative @ $2	20,000	
Total variable expenses		120,000
Contribution margin		80,000
Less fixed expenses:		
Manufacturing overhead	48,000	
Selling and administrative	25,000*	
Total fixed expenses		73,000
Net Income		$ 7,000

*$45,000 − (10,000 units × $2) = $25,000

b.

Direct costing net income	$ 7,000
Add: fixed manufacturing overhead cost deferred in inventory under absorption costing:	
2,000 units x $4*	8,000
Absorption Costing Net Income	$15,000

*$48,000 ÷ 12,000 units produced = $4 per unit.

Chapter 8

Profit Planning

Chapter Study Suggestions

Before reading the chapter material, turn to Exhibit 8-2 and study the flow of budget data as depicted there. This will provide you with an overview of what the chapter contains. Notice particularly how all budgets eventually impact on the cash budget. As suggested by this exhibit, the cash budget is a "key" budget and serves to tie together much of the budget data in an organization. Schedule 8 contains a numerical illustration of a cash budget; it will be helpful to review the contents of this schedule before proceeding with the chapter reading.

Schedules 1 and 2, containing the sales and production budgets, are also of particular importance in understanding the overall budgeting process. As you proceed through the chapter, you will see that all other budgets depend in some way on the sales budget in Schedule 1. Notice that the sales budget is accompanied with a "Schedule of Expected Cash Collections." An understanding of how this schedule is constructed is essential to being able to complete the homework material. The format of the production budget, contained in Schedule 2, should be put to memory.

CHAPTER HIGHLIGHTS AND STUDY GUIDE

A. Profit planning is accomplished through the preparation of a series of documents known as *budgets*. A budget can be defined as a plan for the future expressed in formal quantitative terms.

  1. The master budget is a summary of all phases of a company's plans and goals for the future. It sets specific targets for sales, production, distribution, and financing, and outlines how these targets are to be met.

  2. There are two steps in the budgeting process— planning and control.

    a. Planning involves the development of future objectives and the formulation of steps to achieve these objectives.

    b. Control involves the means by which management assures that all parts of the organization function properly and attain the objectives set down at the planning stage.

  3. There are several advantages to be gained through the use of formal budgeting procedures in an organization.

    a. It forces managers to *think ahead* by requiring them to *formalize* their planning efforts.

    b. It provides definite goals and objectives which serve as *benchmarks* for evaluating subsequent performance.

    c. It uncovers potential *bottlenecks* before they occur.

    d. It *coordinates* the activities of the entire organization by *integrating* the plans and objectives of the various parts.

    e. It provides a vehicle for *communicating* management's plans throughout the entire organization.

B. Much of budgeting rests on the concept of responsibility accounting. Each manager is charged with the control of those costs under his or her care, and his or her performance is measured by how well budgeted goals are met.

  1. Responsibility accounting personalizes the accounting system by looking at costs from a *personal control* standpoint, rather than from an *institutional* standpoint. This concept is central to any effective planning and control system.

  2. A basic premise of the responsibility accounting idea is that effective budget data can be generated as a basis for evaluating managerial performance. The basic purpose of this chapter is to illustrate the steps involved in budget preparation.

C. Budget preparation is a complex task requiring the cooperative effort of all levels of management.

  1. One of the first steps is the choice of a budget period. Operating budgets (the budgets discussed in this chapter) are ordinarily set to cover a one-year period.

    a. The budget year is generally divided into quarters, with the quarters subdivided into months. As the year progresses, budget data are continually reviewed and refined.

    b. These budgets are often set on a continuous or perpetual basis. This is where a new month is constantly being added on the end as the current month is completed. This stabilizes the planning horizon by keeping the budget set at a full 12 months ahead.

  2. Capital budgets, involving the purchase of plant and equipment, have a longer planning horizon, going two or three decades into the future.

  3. The most successful budget programs are those which permit managers to assist in setting the budget data on which their performance is to be evaluated.

    a. When managers participate in this manner, their budgets are said to be *self-imposed* in nature. The major advantage of a self-imposed budget is its positive motivational characteristics. A manager is more apt to work at meeting a budget if he or she has played a central role in its development.

    b. Notice from Exhibit 8-1 that the flow of budget data in an organization is *upward,* rather than from top management downward.

  4. A key element in a successful budgeting program is how top management *uses* budgeted data.

    a. Employees will not be supportive of a budgeting program if it is used as a way of finding someone to "blame" for a problem.

b. The budget must be used as a positive instrument for aiding the company in setting objectives, in measuring results, and in working toward short- and long-range goals.

c. In the past, managers have often been preoccupied with the technical aspects of the budget program to the exclusion of the human aspects. Accountants particularly are open to criticism in this regard.

5. A budget committee, consisting of key executives from the various functional areas, generally has responsibility for overall policy matters relating to the budget program.

D. The master budget is a network consisting of many separate budgets that are interdependent. This network is illustrated in Exhibit 8-2. Study this exhibit carefully before going on.

1. The sales budget is the beginning point in the budgeting process. The sales budget is derived from the *sales forecast*.

a. The sales forecast is broader than the sales budget, generally encompassing potential sales in the entire industry.

b. The sales budget is supported by a "Schedule of Expected Cash Collections," which shows the anticipated cash inflow for the budget period. This is illustrated in Schedule 1 in the text.

2. The sales budget is followed by the production budget, which shows what must be produced to meet both sales needs and inventory needs for the budget period. The formula for the production budget is:

Expected sales in units XXX
Add: Desired ending inventory in units ... XXX
   Total needs XXX
Deduct: Opening inventory in units XXX
Required production in units XXX

The production budget deals with units of *finished goods,* rather than raw materials. Watch this point carefully; it often trips students up as they attempt the homework problems.

3. The direct materials budget follows the production budget, to show the amount of materials which must be acquired to support production and to provide for adequate inventories. The formula for the direct materials budget is:

Raw materials needed to meet the
  production schedule XXXX
Add: Desired ending inventory of
     raw materials XXXX
  Total raw materials needs XXXX
Less: Beginning inventory of raw
     materials XXXX
Raw materials to be purchased XXXX

The direct materials budget should be accompanied by a schedule showing the expected cash disbursements for raw materials for the period.

4. All items of cash inflow or cash outflow appearing on the various budgets are summarized on the cash budget. The cash budget contains four major sections:

    The cash receipts section
    The cash disbursements section
    The cash excess or deficiency section
    The financing section

a. This is one of the key budgets in the planning process. Study the numerical illustrations provided in Schedule 8 with care, noting particularly how the financing section is handled.

b. Notice that the "Total Year" column begins with the cash balance from the first quarter and ends with the cash balance from the fourth quarter.

5. The culmination of the budgeting process is the preparation of an income statement and a balance sheet.

E. Zero-base budgeting is so named because managers using this system are required to start at zero budget levels every year and justify all costs as if the programs involved were being initiated for the first time.

1. This is done in a series of "decision packages" in which the manager ranks all of the activities in his/her department according to relative importance.

2. Opponents of the zero-base approach argue that a zero-base review every year soon becomes mechanical and leads to less cost control, rather than to more cost control.

Appendix: Economic Order Quantity and the Reorder Point

A. There are three groups of costs associated with inventory. They are: the costs of ordering inventory, the costs of carrying inventory, and the costs of not carrying sufficient inventory. In a broad, conceptual sense, the "right" inventory level is that level which will minimize the total of these three classes of costs.

1. Inventory cost minimization has two dimensions—how much to order and how often to do it. The "how much to order" is referred to as the *economic order quantity*.

a. Computing the economic order quantity is a matter of minimizing the first two classes of costs above (the costs of ordering inventory and the costs of carrying inventory).

b. The more frequently orders are placed, the higher the total ordering costs will be, but the lower the total carrying costs will be (since the average inventory balance on hand will be smaller). The reverse will be true if orders are placed less frequently.

c. The formula for finding the order quantity which will minimize ordering and carrying costs is:

$$0 = \sqrt{\frac{2QP}{C}}$$

where: 0 = the order size in units; Q = the annual quantity used in units; P = the cost of placing one order; and C = the annual cost of carrying one unit in stock.

d. The economic production run size can be found by inserting the set-up costs for a new production run in place of the "cost of placing one order" in the formula above.

2. The "how often to place orders" dimension of inventory cost minimization seeks to minimize the total of the second two classes of costs above (the costs of carrying inventory and the costs of not carrying sufficient inventory).

a. This is known as determining the *reorder point*. The formula is:

$$\text{Reorder point} = \frac{\text{Lead time} \times \text{Average daily}}{\text{or weekly usage}}$$

b. The lead time can be defined as the interval between when an order is placed and when the order is finally received from the supplier.

c. If usage during the lead time is not constant, than a *safety stock* must be carried. The safety stock is computed as follows:

Maximum expected usage per day (or week)	XX units
Average usage per day (or week)	XX units
Excess	XX units
Multiply by the lead time	x days (or weeks)
Safety stock	XX units

d. With the safety stock considered, the new formula for computing the reorder point becomes:

$$\text{Reorder point} = \frac{\text{(Lead time} \times \text{Average daily}}{\text{or weekly usage)} + \text{Safety stock}}$$

e. The reorder point and the safety stock are both shown graphically in Exhibit 8-5.

REVIEW AND SELF TEST
Questions and Exercises

True or False

For each of the following statements, enter a T or an F in the blank to indicate whether the statement is true or false.

_____ 1. The best way to establish budget figures is to use last year's actual cost and activity data as this year's budget estimates.

_____ 2. Budgeting is generally of little value to smaller organizations.

_____ 3. The usual starting point in budgeting is to make a forecast of industry sales.

_____ 4. A sales budget and a sales forecast are the same thing.

_____ 5. The master budget is a summary of all phases of a company's plans and goals for the future.

_____ 6. Planning and control are essentially the same thing.

_____ 7. One advantage of budgeting is that it provides definite goals and benchmarks for use in evaluating subsequent performance.

_____ 8. The basic idea behind responsibility accounting is that each manager's performance should be judged by how well he or she manages those items directly under his or her control.

_____ 9. One of the premises underlying the responsibility accounting concept is that effective budget data can be generated as a basis for evaluating performance.

_____ 10. Operating budgets generally have long time horizons and may extend 30 years or more into the future.

_____ 11. A continuous or perpetual budget is one that maintains a constant 12-month planning horizon.

_____ 12. Budget data are generally prepared by top management and distributed downward in an organization.

_____ 13. The budget committee is responsible for preparing detailed budget figures in an organization.

_____ 14. Nearly all other parts of the master budget are dependent in some way on the sales budget.

_____ 15. Ending inventories are primarily a function of an organization not being able to sell all that it had planned to sell during a period.

_____ 16. The primary purpose of the cash budget is to show the expected cash balance at the end of the budget period.

_____ 17. Under zero-base budgeting, a manager is required to start at zero budget levels each period, as if the programs involved were being initiated for the first time.

_____ 18. (Appendix) As inventory levels increase, the costs of carrying inventory will decrease.

_____ 19. (Appendix) In computing the economic order quantity, the manager tries to balance off the costs of ordering inventory and the costs of carrying inventory.

_____ 20. (Appendix) The lead time is a critical factor in computing the reorder point.

Multiple Choice

Choose the best answer or response by placing the identifying letter in the space provided.

_____ 1. A one-year planning horizon is generally used in preparing a(n): a) capital budget; b) operating budget; c) both responses *a* and *b* are correct; d) none of these.

_____ 2. When a manager prepares the budget estimates on which his or her performance is to be evaluated, the budget is said to be: a) zero-based; b) perpetual or continuous; c) self-imposed; d) none of these.

_____ 3. Detailed budget data are generally prepared by: a) the accounting department; b) top management; c) lower levels of management; d) the budget committee; e) none of these.

_____ 4. Most other budgets are dependent in some way on the: a) cash budget; b) budgeted income statement; c) direct materials budget; d) sales budget.

_____ 5. If the beginning cash balance is $15,000, the required ending cash balance is $12,000, cash disbursements are $125,000, and cash collections from customers are $90,000, the company must: a) borrow $32,000; b) borrow $20,000; c) borrow $8,000; d) borrow $38,000; e) none of these.

_____ 6. (Appendix) Computing the economic order quantity is a matter of minimizing the costs of ordering inventory and: a) not carrying sufficient inventory; b) determining the reorder point; c) carrying inventory; d) carrying a safety stock; e) none of these.

_____ 7. (Appendix) The interval between when an order is placed and when the goods are received from the supplier is known as the: a) economic order quantity; b) lead time; c) reorder point; d) none of these.

_____ 8. (Appendix) The reorder point is a function of: a) the economic order quantity; b) the lead time; c) the daily or weekly rate of usage; d) responses *a, b,* and *c* are all correct; e) none of these.

Complete the Statements

Fill in the necessary words to complete the following statements.

1.   In a budgeting program, _____ involves the setting of goals and objectives, and _____ involves the steps taken to assure that the organization meets these goals.

2.   Budgeting provides management with a vehicle for _____ its plans in an orderly way throughout the entire organization.

3.   The accounting concept which looks at costs from a personal control standpoint is called _____ _____.

4.   A _____ or _____ budget maintains a constant 12-month planning horizon, adding a new month on the end when the current month is completed.

5.   A _____-_____ budget contains its own unique system of control, in that if an individual is not able to meet budget specifications, he only has himself to blame.

6.   A standing _____ _____ is charged with overall responsibility for policy matters relating to the budget program.

7.   The sales budget is derived from the _____ _____.

8.   All of the operating budgets, including the sales budget, have an impact of some type on the _____ budget.

9.   Production must be adequate to provide for both sales needs and _____ needs.

10.   (Appendix) There are three groups of costs associated with inventory. These are the costs of _____ inventory, the costs of _____ inventory, and the costs of _____ _____ _____ inventory.

11.   (Appendix) In a broad, conceptual sense, the "right" level of inventory to carry is that which will _____ the total of the three classes of costs in part 10 above.

12.   (Appendix) In order to protect itself against stockouts, an organization should carry an adequate _____ _____, which is computed by taking the difference between average and maximum usage during the lead time.

Exercises

8-1.   Billings Company produces and sells a single product. Expected sales for the next four months are given below:

	Sales in Units
April	10,000
May	12,000
June	15,000
July	9,000

The company needs a production budget for the second quarter. Past experience indicates that end-of-month inventories must equal at least 10 percent of the following month's sales in units. At the end of March, 1,000 units were on hand. Complete the following production budget for the quarter:

	April	May	June	Second Quarter
Budgeted sales				
Add: Desired ending inventory	_____	_____	_____	_____
Total needs				
Deduct: Beginning inventory	_____	_____	_____	_____
Units to be produced	_____	_____	_____	_____

8-2. Dodero Company's production budget for the next four months is given below:

	Production in Units
July	15,000
August	18,000
September	20,000
October	16,000

Five ounces of raw materials are used in the production of each unit of product. At the end of June, 11,250 ounces of material were on hand. The company wants to maintain an inventory of materials equal to 15 percent of the following month's production needs.

Complete the following materials purchases budget for the third quarter:

	July	August	Sept.	Third Quarter
Budgeted production in units				
Raw material needs per unit	___	___	___	___
Production needs in ounces				
Add: Desired ending inventory	___	___	___	___
Total needs in ounces				
Deduct: Beginning inventory	___	___	___	___
Raw materials to be purchased	═══	═══	═══	═══

8-3. Whitefish Company budgets its cash two months at a time. Budgeted cash disbursements for March and April, respectively, follow: for inventory purchases, $90,000 and $82,000; for selling and administrative expenses (includes $5,000 depreciation each month), $75,000 and $70,000; for equipment purchases, $15,000 and $6,000; and for dividend payments, $5,000 and $-0-. Budgeted cash collections from customers are $150,000 and $185,000 for March and April, respectively. The company will begin March with a $10,000 cash balance on hand. A minimum cash balance of $5,000 must be maintained. If needed, the company can borrow money at 12 percent per year. All borrowings are at the beginning of a month, and all repayments are at the end of a month. Interest is paid only when principal is being repaid.

Complete the following cash budget for March and April:

	March	April	Two Months
Cash balance, beginning			
Add: Collections from customers	___	___	___
Total cash available	___	___	___
Less disbursements:			
_____			
_____			
_____			
Total disbursements	___	___	___
Excess (deficiency) of cash available over disbursements	___	___	___
Financing:			
Borrowings (at beginning)			
Repayments (at ending)			
Interest (12% per year)	___	___	___
Total financing	___	___	___
Cash balance, ending	═══	═══	═══

8-4. (Appendix) Glidden Products produces a number of consumer items, including a microwave oven. A vital component part for the ovens is purchased from an outside supplier. In total, the company purchases 2,700 of the parts each year. It costs approximately $15 to place an order, and it costs approximately $.40 to carry one part in inventory for a year. The company works 50 weeks per year.

a.   Compute the economic order quantity for the part, using the following formula:

$$0 = \sqrt{\frac{2QP}{C}} \qquad \text{Where: } 0 = \text{economic order quantity}$$

$$0 = \sqrt{\rule{3cm}{0pt}}$$

$$0 =$$

$$0 =$$

b.   It takes about three weeks to receive an order of parts from the supplier. The company normally uses 54 parts each week in production; usage can be as much as 75 parts per week, however.

Compute the safety stock:

Maximum expected usage per week		parts
Average usage per week		parts
Excess		
Lead time	X	
Safety stock		parts

c.   From the data in parts a and b, compute the reorder point:

Average weekly usage		parts
Lead time	X	
Normal usage		parts
Safety stock		parts
Reorder point		parts

In your own words, explain when and in what quantity orders will be made:

_____

_____

_____

_____

_____

_____

_____

_____

_____

Chapter 8
Answers to Questions and Exercises

True or False

1.	F	6.	F	11.	T	16.	F
2.	F	7.	T	12.	F	17.	T
3.	T	8.	T	13.	F	18.	F
4.	F	9.	T	14.	T	19.	T
5.	T	10.	F	15.	F	20.	T

Multiple Choice

1. b
2. c
3. c
4. d
5. a
6. c
7. b
8. d

Complete the Statements

1. planning, control
2. communicating
3. responsibility accounting
4. continuous, perpetual
5. self-imposed
6. budget committee
7. sales forecast
8. cash
9. inventory
10. ordering, carrying, not carry sufficient
11. minimize
12. safety stock

Exercises

8-1.

	April	May	June	Second Quarter
Budgeted sales	10,000	12,000	15,000	37,000
Add: Desired ending inventory	1,200	1,500	900	900
Total needs	11,200	13,500	15,900	37,900
Deduct: Beginning inventory	1,000	1,200	1,500	1,000
Units to be produced	10,200	12,300	14,400	36,900

8-2.

	July	August	Sept.	Third Quarter
Budgeted production in units	15,000	18,000	20,000	53,000
Raw material needs per unit	x 5 ozs.	x 5 ozs.	x 5 ozs.	x 5 ozs.
Production needs in ounces	75,000	90,000	100,000	265,000
Add: Desired ending inventory-ozs.	13,500	15,000	12,000*	12,000
Total needs in ounces	88,500	105,000	112,000	277,000
Deduct: Beginning inventory-ozs.	11,250	13,500	15,000	11,250
Raw materials to be purchased-ozs.	77,250	91,500	97,000	265,750

*16,000 units (for Oct.) $\times$ 5 ozs. = 80,000 ozs. $\times$ 15% = 12,000 ozs.

8-3.

	March	April	Two Months
Cash balance, beginning	$ 10,000	$ 5,000	$ 10,000
Add: Collections from customers	150,000	185,000	335,000
Total cash available	160,000	190,000	345,000
Less Disbursements:			
For inventory purchases	90,000	82,000	172,000
For selling and administrative expenses	70,000	65,000	135,000
For equipment purchases	15,000	6,000	21,000
For dividends	5,000	--	5,000
Total disbursements	180,000	153,000	333,000
Excess (deficiency) of cash available over cash disbursements	(20,000)	37,000	12,000
Financing:			
Borrowings (at beginning)	25,000	--	25,000
Repayments (at ending)	--	(25,000)	(25,000)
Interest (12% per year)	--	(500)*	(500)
Total financing	25,000	(25,500)	(500)
Cash Balance, ending	$ 5,000	$ 11,500	$ 11,500

*$25,000 × 12% × 2/12 = $500.

8-4. a.

$$ 0 = \sqrt{\frac{2QP}{C}} = \sqrt{\frac{2(2,700)(\$15)}{\$.40}} = \sqrt{202,500} = 450 \text{ parts} $$

b.

Maximum expected usage per week	75 parts
Average usage per week	54 parts
Excess	21 parts
Lead time	x 3 weeks
Safety stock	63 parts

c.

Average weekly usage	54 parts
Lead time	x 3 weeks
Normal usage	162 parts
Safety stock	63 parts
Reorder point	225 parts

Thus, an order for 450 parts will be placed when the stock on hand drops to 225 parts.

Chapter 9

Control through Standard Costs

Chapter Study Suggestions

The first part of the chapter deals with the setting of standard costs. This is important material, since it is easier to understand how standard costs are used if one first understands how they are derived. Exhibit 9-1 presents a *standard cost card,* which is the final product of the standard setting process. You will be using a standard cost card in the homework assignments in both this chapter and in Chapter 10 following, so be sure you understand what a standard cost card contains and how it is constructed.

The last part of the chapter deals with the use of standard costs in variance analysis. Exhibit 9-2 provides an overall perspective of variance analysis, and then Exhibits 9-3, 9-4, and 9-5 give detailed examples of the analysis of materials, labor, and variable overhead. Notice that the figures used in the first part of the chapter to illustrate the setting of standards (see Exhibit 9-1) carry over into Exhibits 9-3, 9-4, and 9-5. As you study, follow the figures from Exhibit 9-1 into the following exhibits. This will help you tie the various parts of the chapter together into one integrated whole. Also, watch the terminology carefully; terms in this chapter are particularly important.

The chapter concludes with a review problem which you should follow through step by step before attempting the homework material.

CHAPTER HIGHLIGHTS AND STUDY GUIDE

A.   A standard can be defined as a benchmark or "norm" for evaluating performance. Standards are found in many facets of day-to-day life.

1. Fast food outlets set quantity standards on the amount of meat going into a sandwich, and auto service centers set time standards on routine service work.

2. The broadest application of the standard idea is found in manufacturing firms, where exacting standards relating to materials, labor, and overhead are developed for each separate product line.

a. These standards are set for both the quantity and the cost of inputs going into manufactured goods.

b. The standards are organized onto a standard cost card, which tells the manager what the final manufactured cost should be for a single unit of product.

c. Actual quantities and costs of inputs are compared against the standards shown on the standard cost card, with any differences brought to the attention of management. This is called *management by exception.*

B.   The initial setting of quantity and cost standards is a vital step in the control process. Standards must be set carefully and accurately if they are to be of maximum use to the manager in cost control.

1. Many persons are involved in the setting of standards, including the accountant, the purchasing agent, the industrial engineer, production supervisors, and line managers.

2. Standards tend to fall into two categories—either ideal or practical.

a. Ideal standards are those that can be attained only by working at top efficiency 100 percent of the time. They allow for no machine breakdowns or lost time.

b. Practical standards, by contrast, allow for breakdowns and normal lost time (such as for coffee breaks). Practical standards are standards which are "tight, but attainable."

c. Most managers feel that practical standards have better motivational characteristics than ideal standards.

d. Throughout the remainder of this book we assume the use of practical, rather than ideal, standards.

3. Direct material standards are set for both the price and quantity of inputs into units of product.

a. Price standards should reflect the final, delivered cost of materials. This price should include freight, handling, and other costs necessary to get the material into a condition ready to use. It should also reflect any cash discounts allowed.

b. Quantity standards should reflect the amount of material going into each finished product, as well as allowances for unavoidable waste, spoilage, and other normal inefficiencies.

4. Direct labor price and quantity standards are usually expressed in terms of labor rate and labor hours.

a. The standard direct labor rate per hour would include not only wages earned but also an allowance for fringe benefits, employment taxes, and other labor-related costs.

b. The standard labor hours per unit should include allowances for coffee breaks, personal needs of employees, clean-up, and machine down time.

5. As with direct labor, the price and quantity standards for variable overhead are generally expressed in terms of rate and hours. The rate represents the variable portion of the predetermined overhead rate.

6. The price and quantity standards for materials, labor, and overhead are summarized on a standard cost card.

a. Study the standard cost card in Exhibit 9-1 with care, and trace the figures in it back through the examples on the preceding pages.

b. Essentially, a standard cost card represents the budgeted cost for a single unit of product.

C.   A number of advantages and disadvantages can be associated with the use of standard costs.

1. Perhaps the most important advantage is that standard costs facilitate the use of "management by exception." Other advantages are cited in the text, and should be reviewed before going on.

2. Perhaps the most important disadvantage is that the use of standard costs can cause a number of behavioral problems in an organization. The nature of these problems is cited in the text, along with other disadvantages, and should be reviewed before going on.

D.   A *variance* is the difference between standard prices and quantities and actual prices and quantities. A general model exists which is very helpful in variance analysis. This model is presented in Exhibit 9-2 in the text.

1. Notice from the model that a price variance and a quantity variance can be computed for all three variable cost inputs—materials, labor, and overhead.

2. Also notice from the model that variance analysis is a matter of input/output analysis.

a. The inputs represent the actual cost or quantity of materials, labor, and overhead used in production; the output represents the good production of the period.

b. The *standard quantity allowed* represents the amount of inputs that *should have been used* in completing the output of the period. This is a key term in the chapter!

3. Exhibit 9-3 shows the variance analysis of direct materials. As you study the exhibit, notice that the center column (Actual Quantity of Inputs, at Standard Price) plays a part in the computation of both the price and quantity variances. This is a key point in variance analysis.

a. The materials price variance can be expressed in formula form as:

$$(AQ \times AP) - (AQ \times SP) = \text{Price variance}$$
$$\text{or}$$
$$AQ (AP - SP) = \text{Price variance}$$

b. Causes of the materials price variance would include excessive freight costs, loss of quantity discounts, improper grade of materials purchased, and rush orders.

c. The materials quantity variance can be expressed in formula form as:

$$(AQ \times SP) - (SQ \times SP) = \text{Quantity variance}$$
$$\text{or}$$
$$SP (AQ - SQ) = \text{Quantity variance}$$

d. Causes of the materials quantity variance would include untrained workers, faulty machines, and improper grade of materials used in production.

e. The materials price variance is generally isolated at the time materials are purchased, whereas the quantity variance is isolated at the time materials are placed into production.

4. Exhibit 9-4 shows the variance analysis of direct labor. Notice that the format is the same as for direct materials, but that in place of the terms "price" and "quantity" the terms "rate" and "hours" are used.

a. The price variance for labor is called a "rate" variance. The formula is:

$$(AH \times AR) - (AH \times SR) = \text{Rate variance}$$
$$\text{or}$$
$$AH (AR - SR) = \text{Rate variance}$$

b. Causes of the rate variance would include misallocation of workers, unplanned overtime, and pay increases.

c. The quantity variance for labor is called an "efficiency" variance. The formula is:

$$(AH \times SR) - (SH \times SR) = \text{Efficiency variance}$$
$$\text{or}$$
$$SR (AH - SH) = \text{Efficiency variance}$$

d. Causes of the efficiency variance would include poorly trained workers, poor quality materials, faulty equipment, and poor supervision.

5. Exhibit 9-5 shows the variance analysis of variable overhead. Notice that the variances are termed "spending" variance and "efficiency" variance. The formulas for these variances are the same as for direct labor.

E.   Not all differences between standard costs and quantities and actual costs and quantities can be termed "exceptions." The manager is interested only in those differences that are significant.

1. Criteria for determining significant variances would include materiality of the item, consistency of occurrence, ability to control the item, and the nature of the item involved.

2. Statistical analysis is often used to determine whether variances are significant and therefore can be termed "exceptions." This is done through use of a statistical control chart, such as is illustrated in Exhibit 9-7.

Appendix: General Ledger Entries to Record Variances

A.   Most companies prefer to make general ledger entries to record variances in the books of account. There are three reasons why this is so:

1. Entry into the accounting records encourages early recognition of variances, thereby facilitating cost control.

2. Entry into the accounting records gives variances a greater emphasis than is possible through informal, out-of-records computations.

3. Entry into the accounting records simplifies the bookkeeping process, by allowing companies to carry inventories at standard cost.

B.   Favorable variances are recorded by credits, and unfavorable variances are recorded by debits in the accounting records.

1. A sample entry to record an unfavorable material price variance would be:

Raw Materials	XX	
Materials Price Variance (unfavorable)	X	
Accounts Payable		XXX

2. A sample entry to record a favorable material quantity variance would be:

Work in Process	XXX	
Materials Quantity Variance (favorable)		X
Raw Materials		XX

3. A sample entry to record direct labor variances would be:

Work in Process	XXX	
Labor Efficiency Variance (unfavorable)	XX	
Labor Rate Variance (favorable)		XX
Wages Payable		XXX

4. Variable overhead variances generally aren't recorded in the accounts separately; rather, they are determined as part of the general analysis of overhead. Overhead analysis is illustrated in Chapter 10.

REVIEW AND SELF TEST
Questions and Exercises

True or False

For each of the following statements, enter a T or an F in the blank to indicate whether the statement is true or false.

_____ 1. Standards play an important part in many aspects of day-to-day life.

_____ 2. The standard cost card tells the manager what the final manufactured cost should be for a single unit of product.

_____ 3. Standard costs are generally determined by analyzing actual costs of prior periods.

_____ 4. Practical standards are generally viewed as having better motivational characteristics than ideal standards.

_____ 5. Ideal standards allow for machine breakdown time and other normal inefficiencies.

_____ 6. In determining a material price standard, the invoice cost should be included, but any freight or handling costs should be excluded.

_____ 7. The material used in rejected or spoiled units of product should be added to good units in computing the standard quantity of material allowed per unit.

_____ 8. The standard rate for variable overhead consists of the variable portion of the predetermined overhead rate.

_____ 9. The difference between a standard and a budget is that a standard is a unit concept, whereas a budget is a total concept.

_____ 10. Raw materials price variances are best isolated when materials are placed into production.

____ 11. Price- and quantity-type variances can be computed for materials, labor and overhead.

____ 12. Waste on the production line will result in a materials price variance.

____ 13. If the actual price or quantity exceeds the standard price or quantity, the variance is unfavorable.

____ 14. Raw materials are generally carried in inventory at standard cost.

____ 15. Labor rate variances are largely out of the control of management.

____ 16. All differences (variances) between standard cost and actual cost should be given attention by management.

____ 17. (Appendix) The use of standard costs simplifies the bookkeeping process.

____ 18. (Appendix) An unfavorable variance would be recorded as a debit in the books of account.

Multiple Choice

Choose the best answer or response by placing the identifying letter in the space provided.

____ 1. The mutual price-quantity variance is usually recognized as part of the: a) price variance; b) quantity variance; c) efficiency variance; d) none of these.

____ 2. It is best to recognize the price variance for raw materials when: a) the materials are placed into production; b) goods are completed and transferred to finished goods; c) the materials are purchased; d) none of these.

____ 3. The labor rate variance is determined by multiplying the difference between the actual labor rate and the standard labor rate by: a) the standard hours allowed; b) the actual hours worked; c) the budgeted hours allowed; d) none of these.

____ 4. If inferior-grade materials are purchased, the result may be: a) an unfavorable materials price variance; b) a favorable materials price variance; c) an unfavorable labor efficiency variance; d) a favorable labor efficiency variance; e) responses *b* and *c* are both correct; f) responses *a* and *d* are both correct.

____ 5. During June, Bradley Company produced 4,000 units of product. The standard cost card indicates the following for labor costs (per unit): 3.5 hours @ $6 = $21. During the month, the company worked 15,000 hours. The standard hours allowed for the month were: a) 14,000 hours; b) 15,000 hours; c) 24,000 hours; d) none of these.

____ 6. The "price" variance for variable overhead is called a: a) rate variance; b) spending variance; c) budget variance; d) none of these.

Complete the Statements

Fill in the necessary words to complete the following statements.

1. In a manufacturing setting, standards are set for both the _____ and _____ of inputs that should go into a unit of product.

2. Standard costs for material, labor, and overhead are summarized on a _____ _____ _____, which tells the manager what the final, manufactured cost should be for a single unit of product.

3. Standards that do not allow for lost time, work interruptions, spoiled units, or machine breakdowns are called _____ standards.

4. _____ standards can be defined as standards that are "tight, but attainable."

5. A standard can be defined as the _____ for a single unit of product.

6. The difference between actual cost and standard cost is called a _____

7. Variance analysis is actually a matter of _____/ _____ analysis. The _____ represents the actual quantity of materials, labor, and overhead used in production, and the _____ represents the good production of the period.

8. The amount of material that *should have been used* to complete the output of the period is called the _____ _____ _____ _____

9. The "price" and "quantity" variances for labor are called the labor _____ variance and the labor _____ variance.

10. Variance analysis through the use of standard costs is one means of implementing the concept of management by _____

Exercises

9-1. Kent Company purchases Klypton in 200 pound cartons, at a cost of $80 per carton. Discount terms of 2/10, n/30 are allowed by the supplier. The freight costs are $130 per average shipment of 25 cartons, which are paid by Kent Company. About 5 percent of the Klypton spoils in the process of shipment. Compute the standard cost per usable pound of Klypton:

> Cost per 200 lb. carton .... $
> Less 2% discount (   ) ....
>   Net cost ....
> Add freight cost (   ) ....
> Total cost per carton .... _____ (a)
>
> Number of usable lbs. per carton:
>   (   ) .... _____ (b)
>
> Cost per usable lb. (a) ÷ (b) .... $ _____

9-2. Selected information relating to Miller Company's operations for April, 19x2 is given below:

Number of units produced	500 units
Number of actual direct labor hours worked	1,400 hours
Total actual direct labor cost	$10,850

The standard cost card indicates that 2.5 hours of direct labor time is allowed per unit, at a rate of $8 per hour.

a.   Complete the following analysis of direct labor cost for the month:

Actual Hours of Input, at the Actual Rate (AH × AR)	Actual Hours of Input, at the Standard Rate (AH × SR)	Standard Hours Allowed for Output, at the Standard Rate (SH × SR)

b. Redo the analysis of direct labor cost for the month, using the following "short-cut" formulas:

$$AH (AR - SR) = \text{Rate variance}$$

$$SR (AH - SH) = \text{Efficiency variance}$$

9-3. The following activity took place in Solo Company during May 19x6:

Number of units produced	450 units
Material purchased	1,500 feet
Material used in production	720 feet
Cost per foot for material purchased	$3

The standard cost card indicates that 1.5 feet of materials are allowed for each unit of product. The standard cost of the materials is $4 per foot.

a. Complete the following analysis of direct materials cost for the month:

Actual Quantity of Inputs, at Actual Price (AQ x AP)	Actual Quantity of Inputs, at Standard Price (AQ x SP)	Standard Quantity Allowed for Output, at Standard Price (SQ x SP)

(A total variance can't be computed in this situation, since the amount of materials purchased differs from the amount of materials used in production.)

b.   Redo the analysis of direct materials cost for the month, using the following "short-cut" formulas:

$$AQ\,(AP - SP) = \text{Price variance}$$

$$SP\,(AQ - SQ) = \text{Quantity variance}$$

9-4. (Appendix) Refer to the data for Solo Company in exercise 9-3 on the previous page. Prepare journal entries to record all activity relating to direct materials for the month:

	Debit	Credit

Chapter 9
Answers to Questions and Exercises

True or False

1. T		7. T		13. T	
2. T		8. T		14. T	
3. F		9. T		15. F	
4. T		10. F		16. F	
5. F		11. T		17. T	
6. F		12. F		18. T	

Multiple Choice

1. a
2. c
3. b
4. e
5. a
6. b

Complete the Statements

1.	cost, quantity	6.	variance
2.	standard cost card	7.	input/output, input, output
3.	ideal	8.	standard quantity allowed
4.	Practical	9.	rate, efficiency
5.	budget	10.	exception

Exercises

9-1.

Cost per 200 lb. carton	$80.00
Less 2% discount ($80.00 × .02)	1.60
Net cost	78.40
Add freight cost ($130 ÷ 25 cartons)	5.20
Total cost per carton	$83.60 (a)

Number of usable lbs. per carton:
(200 lbs. x .95) .... 190 lbs. (b)

Cost per usable lb. (a) ÷ (b) .... $.44

9-2. a.

Actual Hours of Input, at the Actual Rate (AH x AR)	Actual Hours of Input, at the Standard Rate (AH x SR)	Standard Hours Allowed for Output, at the Standard Rate (SH x SR)
$10,850	1,400 hrs. × $8 = $11,200	1,250 hrs.* × $8.00 = $10,000

Rate Variance, $350F	Efficiency Variance, $1,200 U

Total Variance, $850 U

*500 units × 2.5 hrs. = 1,250 hrs.

b.   AH (AR − SR) = Labor Rate Variance
1,400 hrs. ($7.75* − $8.00) = $350F
*$10,850 ÷ 1,400 hrs. = $7.75/hr.

SR (AH − SH) = Labor Efficiency Variance
$8.00 (1,400 hrs. − 1,250 hrs.) = $1,200 U

9-3. a.

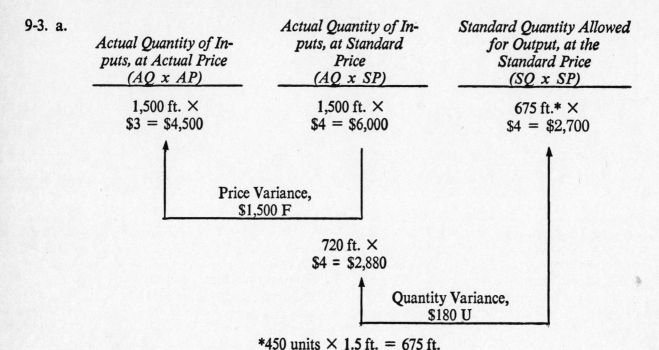

Actual Quantity of Inputs, at Actual Price (AQ x AP)	Actual Quantity of Inputs, at Standard Price (AQ x SP)	Standard Quantity Allowed for Output, at the Standard Price (SQ x SP)
1,500 ft. × $3 = $4,500	1,500 ft. × $4 = $6,000	675 ft.* × $4 = $2,700

Price Variance,
$1,500 F

720 ft. ×
$4 = $2,880

Quantity Variance,
$180 U

*450 units × 1.5 ft. = 675 ft.

b.   AQ (AP − SP) = Materials Price Variance
1,500 ft. ($3 − $4) = $1,500 F

SP (AQ − SQ) = Materials Quantity Variance
$4 (720 ft. − 675 ft.) = $180 U

Notice that a different quantity of materials was purchased (1,500 ft.) than was used in production for the period (720 ft.). This is why a different "AQ" figure is used in the price variance computation than is used in the quantity variance computation.

9-4.
Raw Materials	6,000	
Materials Price Variance		1,500
Accounts Payable		4,500
Work in Process	2,700	
Materials Quantity Variance	180	
Raw Materials		2,880

Chapter 10

Flexible Budgets and Overhead Analysis

Chapter Study Suggestions

The chapter is divided into three parts. The first part covers flexible budgets, with Exhibit 10-8 providing a comprehensive example of how a flexible budget is prepared. As you study the material in this part, pay close attention to the differences that are drawn between a flexible budget and a static budget. These differences are subtle but important.

The middle part of the chapter expands on the variance analysis of variable overhead, by showing how the variable overhead spending and efficiency variances can be organized on a performance report. Exhibits 10-5, 10-6, and 10-7 are the key exhibits here. Notice particularly how the flexible budget data from Exhibit 10-5 ties into the performance reports in Exhibits 10-6 and 10-7 following. This is the key idea in this part of the chapter.

The last part of the chapter covers fixed overhead analysis. Three things here deserve special attention in your study. First, be sure you understand fully what the "denominator activity" is, and how it is used. Second, be sure you understand the difference between an "actual-cost system" and a "standard-cost system," as illustrated in Exhibit 10-9. Third, be sure you understand the variance analysis of fixed overhead illustrated in Exhibit 10-10.

The chapter concludes with a detailed example of flexible budgets and fixed overhead analysis. Follow the example through step by step before attempting the homework material.

CHAPTER HIGHLIGHTS AND STUDY GUIDE

A. The sales budgets, production budgets, and cash budgets which we studied in Chapter 8 are *static* budgets. They are static in the sense that they are geared toward a single level of activity.

    1. The main deficiency of a static budget is that it fails to distinguish between the production control and cost control dimensions of a manager's responsibilities.

        a. Production control means seeing that production goals in terms of output are met.

        b. Cost control means seeing that the output of a period is produced at the least possible cost, consistent with quality standards.

    2. Of these two responsibilities, the static budget does a good job of measuring only how well production goals are being met. The static budget can't be used to measure cost control, since actual activity will rarely coincide with the original static budget level.

B. A flexible budget is geared to a *range* of activity, rather than to a single level. This can be seen from the flexible budget presented in Exhibit 10-3. Notice especially how a "cost formula" is used in the flexible budget.

    1. There are four basic steps involved in preparing a flexible budget:

        a. Determine the relevant range of activity.

        b. Separate costs by their cost behavior patterns (variable, fixed, mixed).

        c. Analyze the mixed costs, as discussed in Chapter 5, by determining their fixed and variable elements.

        d. Using the cost formulas developed in "b" and "c" above, prepare a budget showing what costs will be incurred at various points throughout the relevant range.

    2. The flexible budget is a dynamic tool, in that budgeted costs can be developed to correspond to any actual level of activity within the relevant range.

    3. The activity base underlying the flexible budget must be carefully chosen. Generally, this will be the same base as used in computing predetermined overhead rates (direct labor hours, machine hours, etc.).

    4. Although the term "flexible budget" implies only variable costs, fixed costs are often included as well. This concept is illustrated in Exhibit 10-8 in the text.

        a. One reason for including fixed costs is that the manager may have control over the fixed costs; if so, they should be used in the evaluation of his or her performance.

        b. A second reason for including fixed costs is that the flexible budget is often used as a basis for computing predetermined overhead rates.

C. A performance report for variable overhead can be constructed to show just a spending variance or both a spending and an efficiency variance.

    1. Just a spending variance will be shown on the performance report if budget allowances are based on the actual number of hours worked during the period.

        a. In preparing a performance report, the cost formulas in the flexible budget are applied to the actual number of hours worked for the period.

        b. The budget allowances computed in "a" above are then compared against actual costs of the period and a spending variance results. This concept is illustrated in Exhibit 10-6 in the text.

    2. The overhead spending variance consists of two things: price variations and waste or excessive usage of overhead items.

        a. Thus, the overhead spending variance contains both price and quantity (waste) elements. This makes it different from the price variance for materials and the rate variance for labor.

    3. Both a spending and an efficiency variance will be shown on the performance report if budget allowances are based on both the actual number of hours worked and the standard hours allowed for the output of the period.

        a. A performance report showing both variances is illustrated in Exhibit 10-7. Study the column headings in this exhibit carefully.

        b. The term "overhead efficiency variance" is a misnomer. The inefficiency is really in the *base* underlying the application of overhead.

D. The flexible budget often serves as the basis for computing predetermined overhead rates for product costing purposes.

    1. The predetermined overhead rate formula is:

$$\frac{\text{Estimated manufacturing overhead costs}}{\text{Estimated direct labor hours, etc. (denominator activity)}} = \begin{array}{l}\text{Predetermined}\\\text{overhead}\\\text{rate}\end{array}$$

2. Notice that the estimated activity part of the formula is termed the "denominator activity."

3. Exhibit 10-9 is an extremely important exhibit in Chapter 10. It shows that overhead is applied to work in process differently under a standard-cost system than it is under an actual-cost system.

    a. We studied actual-cost systems in Chapter 3. There we learned that overhead is applied by multiplying the predetermined overhead rate by the actual hours of activity for a period.

    b. By contrast, under a standard-cost system overhead is applied to work in process by multiplying the predetermined overhead rate by the standard hours allowed for the output of the period.

E. Two variances can be computed for fixed overhead—a budget variance and a volume variance.

1. The budget variance represents the difference between actual fixed overhead costs and budgeted fixed overhead costs. The variance can be shown in the following format:

Actual fixed overhead costs .... $XXX
Budgeted fixed overhead costs
  (from the flexible budget) XXX
Budget variance .... $XXX

    a. The fixed overhead budget variance is similar to the variable overhead spending variance.

    b. However, one must keep in mind that fixed costs are often beyond immediate managerial control. When this is true, the budget variance will be largely informational in nature rather than a measure of managerial performance.

2. The volume variance is a measure of utilization of plant facilities. The formula is:

$$\begin{array}{l}\text{Fixed portion}\\\text{of the prede-}\\\text{termined over-}\\\text{head rate}\end{array} \times \left(\begin{array}{c}\text{Denom-}\\\text{inator}\\\text{hours}\end{array} - \begin{array}{c}\text{Stan-}\\\text{dard}\\\text{hours}\end{array}\right) = \begin{array}{l}\text{Volume}\\\text{variance}\end{array}$$

    a. The volume variance does not measure over- or underspending. It is a measure only of plant utilization.

    b. If the denominator activity and the standard hours allowed for the output of the period are the same, then there is no volume variance.

    c. If the denominator activity is greater than the standard hours allowed for the output of the period, then the volume variance is unfavorable.

    d. If the denominator activity is less than the standard hours allowed for the output of the period, then the volume variance is favorable.

REVIEW AND SELF TEST
Questions and Exercises

True or False

For each of the following statements, enter a T or an F in the blank to indicate whether the statement is true or false.

____ 1. A budget prepared for a single level of activity is called a static budget.

____ 2. The only difference between a flexible budget and a static budget is that a flexible budget never contains fixed costs.

____ 3. Although it is effective in measuring production control, a static budget is not effective in measuring cost control.

____ 4. A flexible budget is geared toward a range of activity rather than toward a single level of activity.

____ 5. Direct labor cost would generally be a better base to use in preparing a flexible budget than direct labor hours.

_____ 6. A variable overhead spending variance is affected by waste and excessive usage as well as price differentials.

_____ 7. In variable overhead analysis, the spending variance is generally viewed as being less useful to the manager than the efficiency variance.

_____ 8. The term "overhead efficiency variance" is really a misnomer since this variance has nothing to do with efficiency in the use of overhead.

_____ 9. If overhead is applied to production on a basis of direct labor hours, there will be a close relationship between the labor efficiency variance and the overhead efficiency variance.

_____ 10. Fixed costs should never be included in the flexible budget.

_____ 11. The flexible budget is often used as a basis for preparing the predetermined overhead rate.

_____ 12. The estimated activity figure in the predetermined overhead rate formula is known as the denominator activity.

_____ 13. The denominator activity figure should be changed from month to month as the level of actual activity rises and falls.

_____ 14. Fixed overhead cost should never be included on the standard cost card.

_____ 15. The fixed overhead budget variance is largely beyond the immediate control of management.

_____ 16. The fixed overhead volume variance is a key measure of over- or underspending in an organization.

_____ 17. If the denominator activity figure exceeds the standard hours allowed for the output of a period, one would expect the volume variance to be favorable.

_____ 18. The volume variance is associated with fixed overhead rather than with variable overhead.

Multiple Choice

Choose the best answer or response by placing the identifying letter in the space provided.

_____ 1. In a standard-cost system, overhead is applied to production on a basis of: a) the actual hours required to complete the output of the period; b) the standard hours allowed to complete the output of the period; c) the denominator hours chosen for the period; d) none of these.

_____ 2. A flexible budget: a) is geared to a range of activity; b) excludes fixed costs; c) is conceptually inferior to a static budget; d) none of these.

_____ 3. If the standard hours allowed for the output of a period exceed the denominator hours used in setting overhead rates, there will be: a) a favorable budget variance; b) an unfavorable budget variance; c) a favorable volume variance; d) an unfavorable volume variance; e) none of these.

_____ 4. If a company has a large unfavorable volume variance, one would expect the Manufacturing Overhead account to show: a) underapplied overhead; b) overapplied overhead; c) the volume variance would have no effect on the manufacturing overhead account; d) none of these.

_____ 5. The volume variance is a measure of: a) over- or underspending; b) the difference between actual fixed overhead costs and budgeted fixed overhead costs; c) plant utilization; d) responses a, b, and c are all correct; e) none of these.

_____ 6. When a flexible budget is in use, performance reports can be used effectively to measure: a) production control; b) cost control; c) responses a and b are both correct; d) none of these.

Complete the Statements

Fill in the necessary words to complete the following statements.

1. A production manager has two prime responsibilities to discharge in the performance of his duties— _____ control and _____ control.

2. A budget which is geared to a single level of activity is called a _____ budget.

3. The overhead spending variance is affected as much by _____ as it is by price changes. This is why it is called a "spending" variance.

4. The term "overhead _____ variance" is a misnomer, since it has nothing to do with the _____ of overhead.

5. The expected activity portion of the predetermined overhead rate formula is often called the

_____

6. The _____ is often used as a basis for preparing predetermined overhead rates.

7.   In a _____-cost system, overhead is applied to work in process on a basis of the standard hours allowed for the output of the period.

8.   Two variances can be computed for fixed overhead, a _____ variance and a _____ variance.

9.   If the denominator activity is less than the standard hours allowed for the output of the period, then the _____ variance will be _____

10.   There can be no volume variance for _____ overhead.

Exercises

10-1. Given the following cost formulas for overhead:

Item	Cost Formula
Utilities	$ 6,000 per year, plus $.30 per machine hour
Supplies	$10,000 per year, plus $.80 per machine hour
Depreciation	$25,000 per year
Indirect labor	$21,000 per year, plus $.40 per machine hour
Insurance	$ 8,000 per year

Complete the following flexible budget:

Overhead Costs	Cost Formula	Machine Hours 8,000	10,000	12,000
Variable overhead costs:				
Total variable costs				
Fixed overhead costs:				
Total fixed costs				
Total Overhead Costs				

10-2. Refer to the flexible budget data in Exercise 10-1. The standard time to complete one unit of product is 1.6 machine hours. For the year 19x2 the company budgeted to operate at a 10,000 machine-hour level of activity. During the year the following actual activity took place:

Number of units produced	5,000	units
Actual machine hours worked	8,500	hours

Overhead costs:

Utilities ($6,000 fixed)	$ 8,500
Supplies ($10,000 fixed)	17,000
Indirect labor ($21,000 fixed)	25,000
Depreciation	25,000
Insurance	8,000

Prepare a performance report for 19x2. Show only a spending variance on the report.

Performance Report
For the Year 19x2

Budgeted machine hours ....
Actual machine hours ....
Standard machine hours ....

	Cost Formula	Actual Costs Incurred 8,500 Hrs.	Budget Based on Hrs.	Spending Variance
Variable overhead costs:				
Fixed overhead costs:				
Total Overhead Costs		═══	═══	═══

10-3. The flexible budget for Marina Company is given below:

MARINA COMPANY
Flexible Budget

		Direct Labor Hours		
Overhead Costs	Formula	10,000	12,000	14,000
Variable costs:				
Electricity	$.15/DLH	$ 1,500	$ 1,800	$ 2,100
Indirect materials..........	.50/DLH	5,000	6,000	7,000
Indirect labor	.25/DLH	2,500	3,000	3,500
Total variable costs	$.90/DLH	9,000	10,800	12,600
Fixed costs:				
Depreciation..............		11,500	11,500	11,500
Property taxes		8,500	8,500	8,500
Insurance		4,000	4,000	4,000
Total fixed costs		24,000	24,000	24,000
Total Overhead Costs		$33,000	$34,800	$36,600

A denominator activity level of 12,000 direct labor hours is used in setting predetermined overhead rates. The standard time to complete one unit of product is 1.5 direct labor hours.

For the company's most recent year, the following actual operating data are available:

Units produced	9,000 units
Actual direct labor hours worked	14,000 hours
Actual fixed overhead cost	$23,750

a. Compute the predetermined overhead rate that would be used by the company, and break it down into variable and fixed cost elements:

Predetermined overhead rate ....$_____

Variable cost element ....$_____

Fixed cost element ....$_____

b. How much overhead would have been applied to work
in process during the most recent year? ....$_____
How much of the overhead applied was variable? .....$_____
How much of the overhead applied was fixed? ....$_____

c. Complete the following analysis of fixed overhead cost for the company's most recent year:

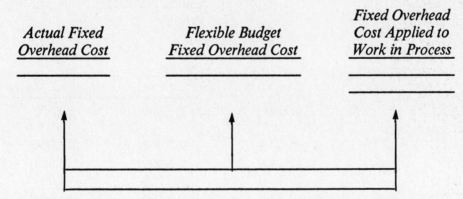

Actual Fixed Overhead Cost	*Flexible Budget Fixed Overhead Cost*	*Fixed Overhead Cost Applied to Work in Process*

d. Redo the variance analysis of fixed overhead, using the following alternate formats:

Actual fixed overhead cost ....$ _____

Budgeted fixed overhead cost .... _____

Budget variance ....$ _____

$$\text{Fixed Portion of the Predetermined Overhead Rate} \times \left(\text{Denominator Hours} - \text{Standard Hours Allowed} \right) = \text{Volume Variance}$$

Chapter 10
Answers to Questions and Exercises

True or False

1.	T	7.	F	13.	F
2.	F	8.	T	14.	F
3.	T	9.	T	15.	T
4.	T	10.	F	16.	F
5.	F	11.	T	17.	F
6.	T	12.	T	18.	T

Multiple Choice

1. b
2. a
3. c
4. a
5. c
6. c

Complete the Statements

1. production, cost
2. static
3. waste
4. efficiency, efficiency
5. denominator activity

6. flexible budget
7. standard
8. budget, volume
9. volume, favorable
10. variable

Exercises

10-1.

Overhead Costs	Cost Formula	Machine Hours		
		8,000	10,000	12,000
Variable overhead costs:				
Utilities	$ .30/MH	$ 2,400	$ 3,000	$ 3,600
Supplies	.80/MH	6,400	8,000	9,600
Indirect labor	.40/MH	3,200	4,000	4,800
Total variable costs	$1.50/MH	12,000	15,000	18,000
Fixed overhead costs:				
Utilities		6,000	6,000	6,000
Supplies		10,000	10,000	10,000
Depreciation		25,000	25,000	25,000
Indirect labor		21,000	21,000	21,000
Insurance		8,000	8,000	8,000
Total fixed costs		70,000	70,000	70,000
Total Overhead Costs		$82,000	$85,000	$88,000

10-2.

Performance Report
For the Year 19x2

Budgeted machine hours	10,000
Actual machine hours	8,500
Standard machine hours	8,000

	Cost Formula	Actual Costs Incurred 8,500 Hrs.	Budget Based on 8,500 Hrs.	Spending Variance
Variable overhead costs:				
Utilities	$ .30/MH	$ 2,500*	$ 2,550	$ (50)
Supplies	.80/MH	7,000	6,800	200
Indirect labor	.40/MH	4,000	3,400	600
Total variable costs	$1.50/MH	13,500	12,750	750
Fixed overhead costs:				
Utilities		6,000	6,000	--
Supplies		10,000	10,000	--
Depreciation		25,000	25,000	--
Indirect labor		21,000	21,000	--
Insurance		8,000	8,000	--
Total fixed costs		70,000	70,000	--
Total Overhead Costs		$83,500	$82,750	$750

*$8,500 − $6,000 = $2,500.

10-3.a.   Predetermined overhead rate: $34,800 ÷ 12,000 DLH = $2.90/DLH

Variable element: $10,800 ÷ 12,000 DLH = $.90/DLH
Fixed element: $24,000 ÷ 12,000 DLH = $2.00/DLH

b.   Overhead applied:

9,000 units × 1.5 hrs./unit = 13,500 standard hours allowed
13,500 standard hours × $2.90 = $39,150 overhead applied

Variable element: 13,500 standard hours × $.90 = $12,150
Fixed element: 13,500 standard hours × $2.00 = $27,000

c.

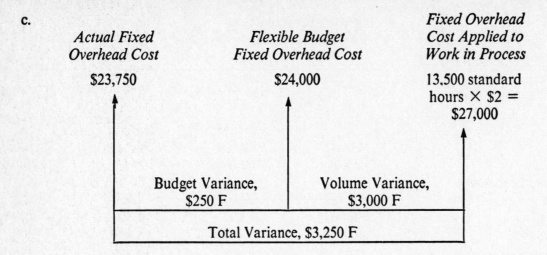

Actual Fixed Overhead Cost	Flexible Budget Fixed Overhead Cost	Fixed Overhead Cost Applied to Work in Process
$23,750	$24,000	13,500 standard hours × $2 = $27,000

Budget Variance, $250 F   Volume Variance, $3,000 F

Total Variance, $3,250 F

d.   Actual fixed overhead cost $23,750
Budgeted fixed overhead cost   24,000
Budget Variance, Favorable .... $ (250)

$2.00 (12,000 hrs. − 13,500 hrs.) = $3,000 F

Control of Decentralized Operations

Chapter Study Suggestions

This chapter is divided into two parts. The first part explains the purpose and operation of a responsibility accounting system. Before you begin your reading, turn to Exhibits 11-2 and 11-3, and study them carefully. These exhibits will give you a perspective of how a responsibility accounting system functions, and make the reading easier. In this part of the chapter formulas are given for computing return on investment (ROI) and residual income. These formulas should be committed to memory, since they are used extensively in the homework material.

The second part of the chapter deals with transfer pricing. A general formula is given for computing a transfer price, which you should learn immediately. In your study, you should spend the bulk of your time on the sections dealing with transfers at market price and at negotiated market price. These are the key sections in this part of the chapter.

CHAPTER HIGHLIGHTS AND STUDY GUIDE

A. The purpose of a responsibility accounting system is to focus attention on the performance of personnel within an organization. Each person who has control over cost or revenue is viewed as being a separate *responsibility center,* on whom a performance report is prepared.

    1. Performance reports build upward, with each manager receiving information on his or her own performance, as well as on the performance of each manager under him or her in the chain of responsibility.

    2. Each manager is charged *only* with those costs over which he or she has control. Exhibit 11-2 shows how reports are structured in a responsibility accounting system. Study this exhibit carefully before going on.

    3. Through a system of performance reports such as shown in Exhibit 11-2, managers at each level of responsibility can see where their time and where their subordinates' time can best be spent in order to control costs and achieve the company's goals.

B. A responsibility accounting system functions best in an organization that is *decentralized.* A decentralized organization is one in which decision making is spread throughout the organization, with managers at all levels making decisions relating to their sphere of responsibility.

C. In a decentralized organization, the responsibility accounting system is structured around a number of centers. These consist of cost centers, profit centers, and investment centers, each of which defines an area of responsibility in the organization.

    1. A cost center is any responsibility center that has control over the incurrence of cost. A cost center has no control over revenues.

    2. A profit center has control over both cost and revenue.

    3. An investment center has control over cost and revenue, and also has control over the use of investment funds. "Investment" represents the investment in plant and equipment, receivables, inventory, and other assets.

D. These concepts of responsibility accounting are very important, since they assist in defining a manager's sphere of responsibility and also in determining how performance will be evaluated, as shown below:

Type of Center	Measure of Performance	Manager Goal
Cost Center	Cost standards or budgets	Minimizing costs in achieving objectives.
Profit Center	Income statement	Maximize net income by meeting sales and cost objectives.
Investment Center	Return on investment	Maximize net income by meeting sales and cost objectives, and do so by fully utilizing investment funds. In other words, maximize ROI.

E. As stated above, performance in an investment center is measured by the return on investment (ROI) formula. The ROI formula is: Margin x Turnover = Return on investment (ROI), where:

$$\text{Margin} = \frac{\text{Net operating income}}{\text{Sales}}$$

$$\text{Turnover} = \frac{\text{Sales}}{\text{Operating assets}}$$

Therefore, the ROI formula becomes:

$$\frac{\text{Net operating income}}{\text{Sales}} \times \frac{\text{Sales}}{\text{Operating assets}} = \text{ROI}$$

The formula can be factored into simpler form as:

$$\frac{\text{Net operating income}}{\text{Operating assets}} = \text{ROI}$$

    1. Net operating income is income before interest and taxes. It is also known as EBIT (earnings before interest and taxes).

    2. Operating assets would include cash, accounts receivable, inventory, and all other assets held for productive use in an organization. Assets common to all divisions (such as assets associated with corporate headquarters) should not be allocated to the divisions in making ROI computations.

F. A company's return on investment can be improved if the manager can either (1) increase sales, (2) reduce expenses, or (3) reduce assets.

G.   Another approach to measuring performance in an investment center is known as *residual income*. Residual income is the net operating income which an investment center is able to earn *above* some minimum rate of return on operating assets.

1.   When residual income is used to measure performance, the purpose is to maximize the total amount of residual income, not to maximize the overall ROI figure.

2.   Residual income is computed as follows:

Average operating assets	$100,000
Net operating income	$ 25,000
Minimum required rate of return is assumed to be 20%.	
20% × $100,000	20,000
Residual income	$ 5,000

3.   Residual income is viewed by some to be a better measure of performance than ROI since it encourages investment in projects that would be rejected under ROI.

4.   A major disadvantage of the residual income approach is that it can't be used to compare divisions of different sizes. The reason is that it can create a bias in favor of the larger divisions, due to the larger numbers involved.

H.   A transfer price is the price charged by one segment of an organization for a good or service which it provides to another segment of the organization. Three general approaches are used in setting transfer prices: (1) set transfer prices at cost, (2) set transfer prices at market price, and (3) set transfer prices at a negotiated market price.

I.   Many firms base transfer prices on cost. This can consist either of the variable costs of the goods being transferred, or fixed costs may also be included, with the transfer price thus based on full (absorption) costs.

1.   Although cost-based transfer prices are widely used, they have a number of disadvantages.

a.   They can lead to dysfunctional decisions in a company, because they have no built-in mechanism for telling the manager when transfers should or should not be made between divisions.

b.   The only division that will show any profits is the one that makes a final sale to an outside party. Other divisions will show no profits for their efforts, and therefore evaluation by the ROI formula, or by the residual income approach, will not be possible.

c.   There is no incentive for the control of costs, since one division simply passes its costs on to the next division.

2.   As a partial offset to these shortcomings, advocates of cost-based transfer prices argue that they are easily understood and highly convenient to use.

3.   If cost-based transfer prices are used, then they should be standard costs, rather than actual costs. This will avoid the passing on of inefficiency from one division to another.

J.   Some form of competitive market price is generally regarded as the best approach to the transfer pricing problem.

1.   The general formula for computing a market-based transfer price is:

$$\text{Transfer price} = \text{Variable costs per unit} + \text{Lost contribution margin per unit on outside sales}$$

2.   Use of market price as a transfer price overcomes the disadvantage listed above in connection with cost-based transfer prices.

3.   In addition to the formula given above, there are certain guidelines that should be followed when using market prices to control transfers between divisions. These guidelines are:

a.   The buying division must purchase internally so long as the selling division meets all bona fide outside prices.

b.   If the selling division does not meet all bona fide outside prices, then the buying division is free to purchase outside.

c.   The selling division must be free to reject internal business if it prefers to sell outside.

d.   An impartial board must be established to arbitrate all disputes over prices.

4. One reason for using market price in transfer pricing is to guard against setting transfer prices below the selling division's opportunity costs. (Opportunity cost can be defined as the potential benefit that is lost or sacrificed when the choice of one course of action requires the giving up of an alternative course of action.)

a. If the selling division is selling all that it can produce to outside customers, then the price which these outside customers are willing to pay is the selling division's opportunity cost.

b. The transfer price which is charged internally can't be less than this opportunity cost, or both the selling division and the company as a whole will suffer a loss of profits. The transfer pricing formula above guards against setting transfer prices below the selling division's opportunity costs.

5. If the selling division has idle capacity, then so long as the transfer price it receives is greater than its variable costs, all parties will benefit by having the buying division purchase inside rather than going outside.

a. If the selling division has idle capacity, and the buying division purchases outside, then suboptimization will result, which means that overall company profitability will be less than it could have been.

b. Where idle capacity exists, the buying and selling divisions will often negotiate a transfer price somewhere between the selling division's variable costs and the current market price.

K.   Sometimes transfer prices are based on a negotiated market price. A negotiated market price is a price agreed upon between the buying and selling divisions that reflects unusual or mitigating circumstances.

1. Possibly the widest use of negotiated market prices is in those situations where no intermediate market price exists. For example, the selling division may produce an item that is not available anywhere else.

2. Negotiated market prices are also used when the selling division has idle capacity, as mentioned above, and when the buying division purchases in large enough quantities to justify a quantity discount.

L.   There is a difficult balance between respecting divisional autonomy in a company and still optimizing profits. The overwhelming experience of multidivisional companies is that divisional autonomy and independent profit responsibility lead to much greater success and profitability than closely-controlled, centrally administered operations.

REVIEW AND SELF TEST
Questions and Exercises

True or False

For each of the following statements, enter a T or an F in the blank to indicate whether the statement is true or false.

_____ 1. Responsibility accounting involves an integrated reporting system that focuses attention on the performance of individual managers within an organization.

_____ 2. In a responsibility accounting system, performance reports start at the bottom and build upward.

_____ 3. Managers have found that a responsibility accounting system functions best in an organization that is highly centralized.

_____ 4. A decentralized organization is one in which decision making is primarily confined to top management.

_____ 5. A segment of an organization having control over the use of investment funds would be termed a profit center.

_____ 6. Excessive funds tied up in operating assets can be just as much of a drag on profits as excessive operating expenses.

_____ 7. Net operating income is income before taxes.

_____ 8. Operating assets would include cash, accounts receivable, inventory, and all other assets presently used in an organization.

____ 9. One way for the manager to improve his or her division's return on investment is to increase the operating assets.

____ 10. Expenses incurred in operating corporate headquarters should be allocated to the separate divisions on the basis of sales dollars.

____ 11. Many managers prefer the residual income approach, because it encourages investments that would be rejected under the ROI approach.

____ 12. Under the residual income approach, the manager seeks to maximize the rate of return on operating assets.

____ 13. The residual income approach is an ideal method of measuring performance in divisions that differ substantially in size.

____ 14. Using "cost" as a transfer price can lead to poor decisions and even to reduced profits in a company.

____ 15. If the selling division is operating at full capacity, the transfer price internally should not be less than the selling price which the division is able to get on outside sales in the intermediate market.

____ 16. If the selling division has idle capacity, then the division's opportunity cost is equal to the price which it is able to get on outside sales in the intermediate market.

Multiple Choice

Choose the best answer or response by placing the identifying letter in the space provided.

____ 1. In a responsibility accounting system: a) all managers are equal in responsibility; b) costs are allocated equally among all managers; c) reports start at the bottom and build upward; d) none of these.

____ 2. If the level of inventory in a company is reduced, and if sales and expenses remain unchanged, one would expect the company's ROI to: a) increase; b) decrease; c) remain unchanged; d) it is impossible to tell what would happen to ROI; e) none of these.

____ 3. The purpose of the residual income approach is to: a) maximize a segment's overall rate of return; b) maximize the total amount of a segment's residual income; c) maximize the return which

a segment is able to get on its operating assets; d) none of these.

____ 4. Transfer prices based on the cost of goods being transferred: a) generally lead to the best long-run transfer pricing decisions; b) must be used if segments are to be evaluated by the ROI formula; c) can result in reduced profits in a company; d) none of these.

____ 5. The market price approach to transfer pricing is designed for use in: a) highly centralized organizations; b) organizations in which little or no autonomy is given to divisional managers; c) organizations which cannot use the return on investment formula; d) none of these.

____ 6. A negotiated market price should be used when: a) the selling division is operating at full capacity, selling all that it can produce in an intermediate market; b) the residual income approach is used to measure divisional performance; c) the selling division is the only supplier of the goods being transferred; d) none of these.

Complete the Statements

Fill in the necessary words to complete the following statements.

1. _____ _____ is a reporting system in which costs are accumulated and reported by levels of responsibility in an organization.

2. A responsibility accounting system functions most effectively in an organization that is highly _____

3. By contrast to a cost center, a _____ center has control over both cost and revenue.

4. The return on investment formula is used to measure performance in a/an _____ center.

5. When being measured by the ROI formula, a manager can improve his or her division's performance by increasing _____, by reducing _____, or by reducing _____

6. It is argued that the _____ _____ approach to performance evaluation encourages managers to make profitable investments that would be rejected by managers being measured by the _____ approach.

7.   The transfer pricing formula states that the transfer price should be equal to the unit _____ _____ of the good being transferred, plus the _____ per unit which is lost to the selling division as a result of giving up outside sales.

8.   Some form of competitive _____ _____ is generally regarded as the best approach to the transfer pricing problem.

9.   If the selling division has _____ _____, then any price which it receives above its variable costs will improve profits for both it and the company as a whole.

10.   _____ is computed by dividing sales by the operating assets.

Exercises

11-1. Fill in the missing information:

| | Company | | |
	1	*2*	*3*
Sales	$750,000	$600,000	$ _____
Net operating income	60,000	_____	27,000
Average operating assets	300,000	200,000	_____
Margin	_____	7.5%	_____
Turnover	_____	_____	1.8
Return on investment (ROI)	_____	_____	27%

11-2. Frankel Company uses the residual income approach to measure performance in its divisions. For the year 19x5, Division A reported the following data: sales, $2,000,000; net operating income, $160,000; average operating assets, $800,000. The company feels that the divisions should earn a minimum return of 16 percent on their assets. Compute Division A's residual income for 19x5:

Net operating income .... $
Minimum required net operating
  income (   ) ....   _____
Residual income .... $ _____

11-3. Perchon Company's Division A produces a small valve that is used by many outside manufacturers as a key part in their products. Cost and sales data relating to the valve are given below:

Selling price per unit $50
Variable costs per unit   30
Fixed costs per unit   12*

*Based on Division A's capacity of 40,000 valves per year.

Perchon Company's Division B is introducing a new product that will use a valve such as the one produced in Division A. An outside supplier has quoted Division B a price of $48 per valve. This represents the normal $50 price, less a quantity discount due to the large number of valves which Division B will be purchasing. Division B would like to purchase the valves from Division A, if an acceptable transfer price can be worked out.

a. Assume that Division A is presently selling all of the valves it can produce to outside customers. Use the transfer pricing formula to determine the transfer price it should quote to Division B:

Transfer price = Variable costs per unit + Lost contribution margin per unit on outside sales

b. Should Division B purchase the valves from Division A or from the outside supplier? Explain.

_____

_____

_____

_____

c. Assume Division B needs 15,000 valves per year. If it purchases the valves from Division A at the price you have computed above, what will be the effect on overall company profits?

_____

_____

_____

_____

d. Refer to the original data. Assume that Division A has ample idle capacity to handle all of Division B's needs. Use the transfer pricing formula to determine the minimum acceptable transfer price between the two divisions.

e. Under the conditions given in "d" above, what is the *maximum* acceptable transfer price between the two divisions? Explain.

_____

_____

_____

_____

Chapter 11
Answers to Questions and Exercises

True or False

1.	T	7.	F	12.	F
2.	T	8.	T	13.	F
3.	F	9.	F	14.	T
4.	F	10.	F	15.	T
5.	F	11.	T	16.	F
6.	T				

Multiple Choice

1. c
2. a
3. b
4. c
5. d
6. c

Complete the Statements

1. Responsibility accounting
2. decentralized
3. profit
4. investment
5. sales; expenses; assets
6. residual income; ROI
7. variable costs; contribution margin
8. market price
9. idle capacity
10. Turnover

Exercises

11-1.

	Company		
	1	*2*	*3*
Sales	$750,000*	$600,000*	$180,000
Net operating income	60,000*	45,000	27,000*
Average operating assets	300,000*	200,000*	100,000
Margin	8%	7.5% *	15%
Turnover	2.5	3	1.8*
Return on investment (ROI)	20%	22.5%	27%*

*Given

11-2.
Net operating income	$160,000
Minimum required net operating income (16% × $800,000)	128,000
Residual income	$ 32,000

11-3.a.   Transfer Price = \$30 + \$20 (\$50 − \$30 = \$20)
Transfer Price = \$50

b.   Division B should purchase the valves from an outside supplier, since the price will be only \$48 per valve, as compared to a price of \$50 internally. Division A can't accept less than \$50 per valve, since it is presently receiving this amount from outside customers. Thus, the \$50 represents Division A's opportunity cost per valve.

c.   Overall company profits will be reduced by \$30,000 per year. Division B will be paying \$2 per valve more than it should be paying, thus reducing the company's profits by a total of \$30,000 per year: \$2 × 15,000 valves = \$30,000.

d.   Transfer Price = \$30 + \$-0- (No lost contribution margin, since Division A has idle capacity.)
Transfer Price = \$30

e.   The maximum acceptable transfer price is \$48 per valve. This is the price that Division B would have to pay to the outside supplier. The \$50 normal price can't be justified, since Division A has idle capacity.

Chapter 12

Pricing of Products and Services

Chapter Study Suggestions

The first part of the chapter discusses the economic framework for pricing. This discussion is designed as background material, so no computations are involved. Simply read through the material with care, noting the new terms as you go.

The real heart of the chapter is contained in the sections dealing with standard pricing, new product pricing, and special pricing decisions. In the first of these sections (Pricing Standard Products), study Exhibits 12-3 and 12-5 carefully. These exhibits show how alternate price quotation sheets are prepared, using cost-plus pricing. This section also contains formulas for computing the markup added to products. These formulas are used repeatedly in the homework, so you should commit them to memory.

In the section titled, Pricing New Products, be sure you understand how target costs are computed. The computation involved here looks simple, but students often foul it up on exams. Finally, you must thoroughly understand how special pricing decisions are made. Study and then restudy this material, noting the pricing model contained in Exhibit 12-8. Be sure you understand the function of the "floor," the "ceiling," and the "range of flexibility" as shown in this exhibit.

CHAPTER HIGHLIGHTS AND STUDY GUIDE

A.   Economic theory contains a broad conceptual framework which is helpful to the manager in his or her pricing decisions.

1. Microeconomic theory states that the best price to charge for a product is that price which maximizes the difference between total revenue and total costs.

a. Total revenue represents the total dollars received by a firm for various quantities sold. The economist assumes that it is not possible to sell an unlimited number of units at the same price. For this reason, the total revenue curve tends to flatten out as volume increases, as shown in Exhibit 12-1.

b. Total cost represents the total dollars expended to produce various quantities sold. As long as the rate of increase in revenue for additional units sold is greater than the rate of increase in total cost, the company can profit by producing and selling more units of product.

2. The optimum price to charge for a product can also be determined from the intersection of the marginal revenue and the marginal cost curves.

a. Marginal revenue is the addition to total revenue resulting from the sale of one additional unit of product. Marginal cost is the addition to total cost resulting from the production and sale of one additional unit of product.

b. The optimum price to charge for a product is where marginal revenue and marginal cost are equal, as shown in Exhibit 12-2.

3. Price elasticity measures the degree to which volume of sales is affected by a change in price per unit.

a. Demand is price inelastic if a change in price has little or no effect on the volume of units sold. Demand is price elastic if a change in price has a substantial effect on the volume of units sold.

b. Cross-elasticity measures the degree to which demand for one product is affected by a change in price for a substitute product.

4. The general economic models provide only broad, conceptual guidelines in pricing decisions, and therefore have limitations in their use. These limitations are:

a. Cost and revenue data available often provide only approximations of the shape of the revenue and cost curves depicted in the economist's models.

b. The models are applicable only under specified economic conditions. Some of these are: monopoly, monopolistic competition, and oligopoly. Note the definition of these terms in the text.

c. Price is just one element in the marketing of a product. Other important factors are product design, distribution channels, and intensity of selling effort.

d. Businesses do not always seek to maximize profits. Due to pressures from society, they may seek only to earn a "satisfactory" profit.

B.   In pricing standard products the key concept is to recognize that selling prices must be sufficient in the long run to cover all costs of the firm, both variable and fixed, as well as to provide for a reasonable return on the stockholders' investment.

1. The most common approach to the pricing of standard products is to employ some type of cost-plus pricing formula. Under this method a cost base is computed, to which a markup is added in order to arrive at a target selling price.

2. Cost-plus pricing can be used to compute a target selling price by either the absorption approach or the contribution approach.

a. The absorption approach defines the cost base as the cost to produce one unit of product. Selling and administrative costs are not included in this cost base, but rather are provided for through the markup which is added on to arrive at the target selling price. The format is:

Unit cost to manufacture	$50
Markup to cover selling and administrative expenses, and desired profit—	
40% of cost to manufacture	20
Target selling price	$70

b. The contribution approach defines the cost base in terms of variable production, selling, and administrative expenses. A markup designed to cover appropriate fixed costs and to provide the desired profit element is added to this variable cost base. The format is:

Variable manufacturing costs	$35
Variable selling and administrative expenses	5
Total variable expenses	40
Markup to cover fixed expenses and desired profit—75% of variable expenses	30
Target selling price	$70

c. In both cases above, the term "cost-plus" is a misnomer, since part of the costs are buried in the "plus" or markup part of the formula. For the absorption approach, these are the selling and administrative expenses; for the contribution approach, these are the fixed costs.

3. By far the most crucial element in the cost-plus pricing formulas is the percentage markup added to the cost base. This is because it must be sufficient to cover a portion of the costs of the firm, and to provide for the desired profit element.

a. One approach to determining the markup to add to products is to base the markup on some desired return on investment (ROI). A formula exists which can be used to determine the appropriate markup percentage, given the ROI figure which management wishes to achieve.

b. If absorption costing is being used, the formula is:

$$\text{Markup Percentage} = \frac{\text{Desired Return on Assets Employed} + \text{Selling and Administrative Expenses}}{\text{Volume in Units} \times \text{Unit Cost to Manufacture}}$$

c. If the contribution approach is being used, the formula is:

$$\text{Markup Percentage} = \frac{\text{Desired Return on Assets Employed} + \text{Fixed Costs}}{\text{Volume in Units} \times \text{Unit Variable Expenses}}$$

4. Rather than compute prices by means of a cost-plus formula, some companies use an alternative approach called time and material pricing. Under this method two pricing rates are established—one based on direct labor time and a second based on direct material used.

a. The time component is typically expressed as a labor rate per hour. The rate is computed by adding together three elements: (1) the direct costs of the employee, including salary and fringe benefits; (2) an allowance for selling, administrative, and other expenses of the company; and (3) an allowance for a desired profit.

b. The material component is determined by adding a material loading charge to the invoice cost of the materials used on the job. This charge is designed to cover the costs of ordering, handling, and carrying materials in stock, plus a profit margin on the materials.

c. Time and material pricing is typically used by service organizations, ranging from doctors' offices to TV repair shops.

C. The pricing of new products is the most difficult of all pricing decisions, because of the uncertainties involved. To alleviate some of the uncertainty, the company may test market its product to see how well the product's price is accepted by consumers.

1. The two basic pricing strategies for new products are:

a. Skimming pricing—this approach involves setting a high initial price for a new product, with a progressive lowering of the price as time passes and as the market broadens and matures. This approach maximizes short-run profits.

b. Penetration pricing—this approach involves setting low initial prices in order to gain quick acceptance in a broad portion of the market.

2. When introducing a new product, the company often will know what price should be charged, and the problem will be to develop a product that can be sold profitably at that price. The company's approach will be to set *target costs* that can be used as guides in developing a product that can be sold within the desired price range.

D. Special pricing decisions can arise for both standard products and products not normally produced by a firm. In special pricing situations, the contribution approach to pricing tends to yield better results than the absorption approach.

1. The reason the contribution approach yields better results is that it organizes cost in a way that is compatible with cost-volume-profit concepts, and it provides a ready framework within which the price setter can operate.

2. This framework is presented in general model form in Exhibit 12-8. Study this exhibit with care, noting the function of the floor, the ceiling, and the range of flexibility.

3. The model in Exhibit 12-8 is appropriate only in special pricing situations, since it results in a selling price which is based only on variable costs. The model is appropriate for setting prices under three conditions:

a. When idle capacity exists.

b. When operating under stress conditions, such as when the market for a product is severely depressed and large stocks are on hand.

c. When faced with sharp competition under a competitive bidding situation.

E. In pricing decisions, firms must take care to keep their actions within the requirements of the Robinson-Patman Act. The act forbids quoting different prices to competing customers unless the difference in pricing can be traced to differences in cost to manufacture, to sell, or to deliver the product.

REVIEW AND SELF TEST
Questions and Exercises

True or False

For each of the following statements, enter a T or an F in the blank to indicate whether the statement is true or false.

_____ 1. The optimal selling price for a product is that point where marginal revenue is equal to marginal cost.

_____ 2. The economist's marginal cost concept is basically the same as the accountant's incremental cost concept.

_____ 3. Demand for a product is price inelastic if a change in price has little or no effect on the volume of units sold.

_____ 4. In pricing standard products, the key factor is to set the selling price high enough to cover all variable costs plus provide for a desired profit.

_____ 5. In cost-plus pricing, the cost base is generally the same under either the absorption or the contribution approach; however, the percentage markup is generally different.

_____ 6. The contribution approach to cost-plus pricing defines the cost base in terms of a product's variable costs, including variable selling and administrative expenses.

_____ 7. If a company has a 20 percent desired ROI, then it should add a 20 percent markup to its products.

_____ 8. Time and material pricing is more appropriate to service-type organizations than to manufacturing firms.

_____ 9. In time and material pricing, the material loading charge includes a profit element.

_____ 10. The purpose of penetration pricing is to maximize short-run profits.

_____ 11. Even though markup percentages may differ, the same target selling price can be obtained using either the absorption approach or the contribution approach to cost-plus pricing.

_____ 12. In special pricing situations, so long as the price received on added business exceeds the variable costs (and any incremental fixed costs), overall net income will be increased by utilizing idle capacity.

_____ 13. Most firms seek to earn a "satisfactory" profit, rather than to maximize profits.

_____ 14. Fixed costs are not considered in long-run pricing decisions.

_____ 15. The markup in cost-plus pricing consists of the desired profit of the firm.

Multiple Choice

Choose the best answer or response by placing the identifying letter in the space provided.

_____ 1. If demand for a product is price elastic: a) then the product has few substitutes; b) then a change in price will have little effect on the volume of units sold; c) then a change in price will have substantial effect on the volume of units sold; d) none of these.

_____ 2. Under the absorption approach to cost-plus pricing, the markup is designed to cover: a) the variable selling and administrative expenses; b) the fixed selling and administrative expenses; c) a desired profit to the company; d) all of the above; e) none of the above.

_____ 3. The economic situation where a few large sellers compete directly with each other is called: a) monopoly; b) monopolistic competition; c) oligopoly; d) none of these.

_____ 4. The setting of a low initial price in order to gain quick acceptance in a broad portion of the market is called: a) penetration pricing; b) skimming pricing; c) variable pricing; d) none of these.

_____ 5. Under the contribution approach to pricing, the floor in the range of flexibility consists of: a) the fixed costs; b) the variable costs; c) the target selling price; d) none of these.

_____ 6. Under the contribution approach to cost-plus pricing, in addition to providing a desired profit element, the markup is designed to cover: a) the variable costs; b) the selling and administrative expenses; c) the fixed costs; d) none of these.

Complete the Statements

Fill in the necessary words to complete the following statements.

1. Demand for a product is price _____ if a change in price has little or no effect on the volume of units sold.

2. Under the _____ approach to cost-plus pricing, the cost base is defined as the cost to produce one unit of product.

3. _____ _____ is the addition to total cost resulting from the production and sale of one additional unit of product.

4. By far the most crucial element in the cost-plus pricing formulas is the percentage _____ added to the cost base.

5. One of the most common ways to determine the percentage markup which should be added to products is to base the markup on the company's desired _____ ___ _____

6. Under time and material pricing, the material component is determined by adding a _____ _____ _____ to the invoice cost of any materials used on the job.

7. _____ pricing is most effective in those markets where entry is relatively difficult, because of the technology or investment required.

8. The contribution approach to pricing provides a _____ and a _____ between which the price setter operates in special pricing decisions.

9. In special pricing decisions using the contribution approach, the manager can move within the _____ ___ _____ as far down as the floor of variable costs in quoting a price to a prospective customer.

10. Under the contribution approach to cost-plus pricing, the _____ costs are included as part of the markup which is added to the cost base.

Exercises

12-1. Manufacturing costs and other costs relating to a product produced by Mackey Company are given below:

Direct materials	$10
Direct labor	12
Variable overhead	1
Fixed overhead	7
Variable selling and administrative	2
Fixed selling and administrative	3

a.   Assume that the company uses the absorption approach to cost-plus pricing, and adds a 50% markup to obtain target selling prices. Compute the target selling price for the product above.

_____ $

_____

_____

_____   ____

    Total cost to manufacture

Markup—50% × $_____

Target selling price $____

b.   Assume that the company uses the contribution approach to cost-plus pricing, and adds an 80% markup to obtain target selling prices. Compute the target selling price for the product above.

_____ $

_____

_____

_____   ____

    Total variable expenses

Markup—80% × $_____

Target selling price $____

12-2. a.   Speckart Company has determined that an investment of $800,000 is needed in order to produce and market 30,000 units of Product A each year. The company's cost accountant estimates that it will cost $50 to manufacture a unit of Product A at a 30,000-unit level of activity, and that selling and administrative expenses will total $400,000 per year. Compute the required markup percentage for Product A, assuming that the company uses the absorption approach to costing, and has a 25% desired ROI.

$$\text{Markup Percentage} = \frac{\text{Desired Return on Assets Employed} + \text{Selling and Administrative Expenses}}{\text{Volume in Units} \times \text{Unit cost to Manufacture}}$$

Markup Percentage =

b. Hansen Company has determined that an investment of $750,000 is needed in order to produce and market 25,000 units of Product B each year. The company estimates that variable costs associated with Product B will total $24 per unit, and that fixed costs will total $300,000 per year. Compute the required markup percentage for Product B, assuming that the company uses the contribution approach to costing, and has a 20% desired ROI.

$$\text{Markup Percentage} = \frac{\text{Desired Return on Assets Employed} + \text{Fixed Costs}}{\text{Volume in Units} \times \text{Unit variable Expenses}}$$

$$\text{Markup Percentage} =$$

12-3. A price quotation sheet, using the contribution approach, is given below:

Direct materials	$15
Direct labor	10
Variable overhead	3
Variable selling and administrative	2
Total variable expenses	$30
Markup—60% x $30	18
Target selling price	$48

Identify the "floor," the "ceiling," and the "range of flexibility" on this quotation sheet. If the company has excess capacity and is offered a price of $39 per unit on a special order, should it accept or reject the offer? Explain.

_____

_____

_____

_____

_____

_____

Chapter 12
Answers to Questions and Exercises

True or False

1.	T	6.	T	11.	T
2.	T	7.	F	12.	T
3.	T	8.	T	13.	T
4.	F	9.	T	14.	F
5.	F	10.	F	15.	F

Multiple Choice

1. c
2. d
3. c
4. a
5. b
6. c

Complete the Statements

1. inelastic
2. absorption
3. Marginal cost
4. markup
5. return on investment
6. material loading charge
7. Skimming
8. ceiling; floor
9. range of flexibility
10. fixed

Exercises

12-1. a.
Direct materials	$10
Direct labor	12
Variable overhead	1
Fixed overhead	7
Total cost to manufacture	$30
Markup—50% x $30	15
Target selling price	$45

b.
Direct materials	$10
Direct labor	12
Variable overhead	1
Variable selling and administrative	2
Total variable costs	$25
Markup—80% x $25	20
Target selling price	$45

12-2. a.   Markup Percentage $= \dfrac{(25\% \times \$800{,}000) + \$400{,}000}{30{,}000 \text{ units} \times \$50}$

$= \dfrac{\$600{,}000}{\$1{,}500{,}000}$

$= 40\%$

b.   Markup Percentage $= \dfrac{(20\% \times \$750{,}000) + \$300{,}000}{25{,}000 \text{ units} \times \$24}$

$= \dfrac{\$450{,}000}{\$600{,}000}$

$= 75\%$

12-3.

Direct materials	$15
Direct labor	10
Variable overhead	3
Variable selling and administrative	2
Total variable expenses	$30 Floor
Markup—60% x $30	18
Target selling price	$48 Ceiling

Range of Flexibility

The company should accept the $39 offer. This figure is within the range of flexibility, and is $9 above the floor of variable costs. Thus, it will add $9 per unit contribution margin to the company for each unit sold in the special order.

Chapter 13

Relevant Costs for Decision Making

Chapter Study Suggestions

In the first few pages of the chapter, guidelines are given for identifying relevant costs. Study these pages carefully, since these guidelines are used many times in the remaining pages of the chapter to show how relevant costs can be identified in various decision-making situations.

Three decision-making situations identified in the chapter are of particular importance. These are (1) adding and dropping line products, (2) make or buy, and (3) sell or process further. Concentrate your study on Exhibits 13-3, 13-5, and 13-7, which deal with these three topics. You must have a thorough understanding of the analytical procedure followed in each of these exhibits in order to be able to do the homework material.

CHAPTER HIGHLIGHTS AND STUDY GUIDE

A. A relevant cost can be defined as a cost which is applicable to a particular decision in the sense that it will have a bearing on which alternative the manager selects.

1. All costs are relevant in decision making except costs which are not avoidable. Costs which are not avoidable fall into two categories: (a) sunk costs, and (b) future costs which do not differ between alternatives.

2. The relevant costs in a decision can also be identified as those costs (and revenues) which are differential between the alternatives being considered.

3. To identify those costs which are differential and therefore relevant, the manager should take the following steps:

a. Assemble *all* costs associated with *each* alternative being considered.

b. Eliminate those costs which are sunk.

c. Eliminate those costs which do not differ between alternatives.

d. Make a decision based on the remaining cost data. These will be the differential or avoidable costs, and hence the costs relevant to the decision to be made.

4. Costs which are relevant in one situation may not be relevant in another situation. Simply put, this means that the manager needs different costs for different purposes.

B. Sunk costs are never relevant in decision making since they are not avoidable.

1. The book value of (and depreciation on) old equipment represents a sunk cost. Hence, it is not relevant in decision making.

2. However, we must note that depreciation is a sunk cost *only* if it relates to old equipment (e.g., equipment which has already been purchased). Thus, depreciation on *new* equipment would be a relevant cost in decision making.

C. Future costs that do not differ between alternatives are not relevant costs.

1. For example, Hewlett Company is considering the purchase of Machine A or Machine B. Main-tenance costs will be the same regardless of which machine is purchased. Thus, maintenance costs are irrelevant to the choice between the machines, since they will be of no help in determining which machine should be purchased.

2. Relevant costs should be isolated in cost analysis for two reasons:

a. Only rarely will enough information be available to prepare a detailed income statement such as those illustrated in the chapter. Typically, only limited data are available; therefore, the decision maker *must* know how to recognize which costs are relevant and which are not.

b. The use of irrelevant costs intermingled with relevant costs may draw the decision maker's attention away from the matters that are really critical to the problem being studied.

D. Adding or dropping product lines is a difficult problem with which management is confronted. Study the detailed example provided in the section titled, "Adding and Dropping Product Lines."

1. Notice that costs are classified as being either "avoidable" or "not avoidable" according to the guidelines given earlier.

2. In deciding whether a product line should be retained or dropped:

a. If the contribution margin which will be lost by dropping a product line is *greater* than the costs which will be avoided, then the product line should be retained.

b. If the contribution margin which will be lost by dropping a product line is *less* than the costs which will be avoided, then the line should be dropped.

3. An alternate approach to deciding whether to retain or drop a product line or other segment of a company is found in Exhibit 13-3. In this approach two income statements are prepared: one showing present operations, and another showing what costs and revenues would be if the product line was dropped. Study Exhibit 13-3 to see how this analysis is organized.

4. The decision to keep or drop a product line or other segment of a company is often clouded by the allocation of common fixed costs.

a. Such allocations can make a product line or other segment *appear* to be unprofitable, when in fact the product line may be contributing substantially to the overall profits of the company.

b. Common fixed costs should never be allocated to segments of a company; segments should be charged only with those costs which are directly traceable to them, as shown in Exhibit 13-4.

E. A decision to produce a particular part internally, rather than to buy the part externally from a supplier, is often called a "make or buy" decision. "Make or buy" really relates to vertical integration in a company. When a company is involved in more than one of the steps from the extracting of raw material to the fabrication of a finished product, it is said to be vertically integrated.

1. There are several advantages to vertical integration. These include (a) less dependence on suppliers, (b) assurance of quality control of products, and (c) cost savings made possible by "making" rather than "buying."

2. The disadvantages of integration include: (a) severance of existing suppliers may disrupt long-run relationships, (b) if the firm needs goods from former suppliers, the former suppliers may be uncooperative, (c) changing technology may make continued production of one's own parts more costly than purchasing from the outside.

3. An example of make or buy is contained in the text, in Exhibit 13-5. Notice from the exhibit that the costs which are relevant in a make or buy decision are those costs which are *differential* as between the make or buy alternatives.

4. Opportunity cost is a key factor in a make or buy decision.

a. If there are no alternative uses of facilities currently being used to make a part or a product, then opportunity cost is zero and it does not need to be considered in make or buy computations

b. On the other hand, if buying from outside the company would free up facilities or time which could be used to produce some new product, then an opportunity cost is present. This opportunity cost is the segment margin which could be obtained from the new product; it becomes part of the cost of the "make" alternative in a make or buy decision.

F. There are scarce resources in every firm. The scarce resource might be floor space, labor time available, machine time available, or advertising space available.

1. To maximize total contribution margin, firms may not necessarily want to promote those products that have the highest individual contribution margins. Rather, total contribution margin will be maximized by promoting those products that promise the greatest contribution margin in relation to the scarce resources of the firm.

2. The manager should compute contribution margin for products in terms of the amount generated per unit of scarce resource, and use this as a guide to which products should be produced and sold.

G. The manufacturing processes of some firms are such that several end products are produced from a single raw material input. Such products are known as *joint products,* with the common input from which they are derived known as the *joint product cost.* The *split-off point* is that point in the manufacturing process at which the joint products can be recognized as individual units of output.

1. Decisions as to whether a joint product should be sold at the split-off point or processed further and then sold are known as "sell or process further" decisions.

2. Joint product costs incurred up to the split-off point are irrelevant in decisions regarding whether or not a product should be processed further, since they are sunk costs.

3. It will always be profitable to continue processing joint products after the split-off point *so long as the incremental revenue from such processing exceeds the incremental processing costs.* An example of a "sell or process further" analysis is provided in Exhibit 13-7.

Appendix: Linear Programming

A. Linear programming is a mathematical tool designed to assist management in making decisions in those situations where constraining or limiting factors are present. Linear programming seeks to identify the "right" mix of products that will maximize profits, given the limiting factors (scarce resources) faced by a firm.

1. A graphical approach can be used to solve a linear programming problem in those situations where only two products are involved.

2. The four basic steps in a linear programming graphical analysis are:

   a. Determine the objective function and express it in algebraic terms.

   b. Determine the constraints under which the firm must operate and express them in algebraic terms.

   c. Determine the feasible production area on a graph. This area will be bounded by the constraint equations derived in "b" above, after the constraint equations have been expressed on the graph in linear form.

   d. Determine from the feasible production area that mix of products which will maximize (or minimize) the objective function.

3. The objective function represents the goal which is to be achieved, expressed in terms of the variables involved. The goal might be to maximize total contribution margin or it might be to minimize total cost.

4. Constraint equations are algebraic representations of the constraints under which the firm must operate. These constraints may be raw material, machine hours, labor hours, product demand, etc.

5. The feasible production area is formed by the constraint equations on the graph. The firm could operate *anywhere* within the feasible production area.

6. The optimal product mix will always fall on a corner of the feasible production area.

7. In the graphical representation of constraints, the following should be remembered:

   a. If the constraint equation is stated in terms of less than or equal to ($\leqslant$), the direction of the constraint will be *inward* toward the origin of the graph.

   b. If the constraint equation is stated in terms of greater than or equal to ($\geqslant$), the direction of the constraint will be *outward* away from the origin of the graph.

8. The *simplex* method is a more complex approach to solving linear programming problems than is the graphical method. The simplex method is used in those situations where *more than* two products are involved.

9. Linear programming has been successfully used in many areas of our economy where multiple constraints exist.

REVIEW AND SELF TEST
Questions and Exercises

True or False

For each of the following statements, enter a T or an F in the blank to indicate whether the statement is true or false.

_____ 1. All costs are relevant in decision making, except those costs which are not avoidable.

_____ 2. Variable costs are relevant costs in decision making, whereas fixed costs are not relevant.

_____ 3. A sunk cost is an avoidable cost.

_____ 4. Depreciation is a relevant cost if it relates to equipment which has not yet been purchased.

_____ 5. Future costs are relevant in a decision if the same costs will be sustained regardless of which alternative is selected.

_____ 6. Costs which are relevant in one decision situation are not necessarily relevant in another decision situation.

_____ 7. One way to define relevant costs is to say that they are costs which are avoidable.

_____ 8. If by dropping a product line a company is able to avoid more in fixed costs than it loses in contribution margin, then it will be better off if the line is eliminated.

_____ 9. Allocation of common fixed costs to product lines and to other segments of a company helps the manager to see if the product line or segment is profitable.

_____ 10. If a product line has a negative segment margin, it is conclusive evidence that the product line should be discontinued.

_____ 11. Opportunity cost is a key factor in a make or buy decision.

_____ 12. A company should always promote that product which has the highest contribution margin per unit sold.

_____ 13. A joint product should continue to be processed after the split-off point so long as the incremental revenue from such processing exceeds the incremental processing costs.

_____ 14. Joint product costs are irrelevant in decisions regarding what to do with joint products after the split-off point.

_____ 15. (Appendix) The purpose of linear programming is to help management make decisions in those situations where constraining or limiting factors are present.

_____ 16. (Appendix) The objective function equation expresses the constraints under which the firm must operate.

_____ 17. (Appendix) The feasible production area is bounded by the lines of the constraint equations.

_____ 18. (Appendix) The corners of the feasible production area are the points where the optimal product mix can be found that will maximize profits.

Multiple Choice

Choose the best answer or response by placing the identifying letter in the space provided.

_____ 1. Depreciation is a relevant cost in decision making if: a) the depreciation relates to equipment already on hand; b) the depreciation relates to equipment which has not yet been purchased; c) depreciation is never relevant in decision making; d) none of these.

_____ 2. One of Simplex Company's product lines has a contribution margin of $50,000 and fixed costs totaling $60,000. If the product line is dropped, $20,000 in fixed costs can be avoided. As a result of dropping the product line, the company's net income should: a) decrease by $50,000 per period; b) increase by $30,000 each period; c) decrease by $30,000 each period; d) increase by $10,000 each period; e) none of these.

_____ 3. Allocated common costs: a) are necessary in order to determine the profitability of a product line; b) are always relevant in decision making; c) are sometimes relevant in decision making; d) are never relevant in decision making; e) none of these.

_____ 4. All costs are relevant in decision making, except sunk costs and: a) fixed costs; b) future costs that differ between alternatives; c) avoidable costs; d) future costs that do not differ between alternatives; e) none of these.

_____ 5. Product A has a contribution margin of $8 per unit, a contribution margin ratio of 50 percent, and requires 4 machine-hours to produce. Product B has a contribution margin of $12 per unit, a contribution margin ratio of 40 percent, and requires 5 machine-hours to produce. If the company has limited machine-hours available, then it should produce and sell: a) Product A since it has the highest contribution margin ratio; b) Product B since it has the highest contribution margin per machine-hour; c) Product A since it requires fewer machine-hours per unit than does Product B; d) Product B since it has the highest contribution margin per unit; e) none of these.

_____ 6. Products A and B are joint products. Product A can be sold for $1,200 at the split-off point, or be processed further at a cost of $600 and then sold for $1,700. Product B can be sold for $3,000 at the split-off point, or be processed further at a cost of $800 and then sold for $4,000. The company should process further: a) Product A; b) Product B; c) both products; d) none of these.

_____ 7. (Appendix) A company produces two products, X and Y. The contribution margin per unit of X is $15, and the contribution margin per unit of Y is $12. The company has 60 hours of production time available each period, and it takes 4 hours to produce one unit of X and 7 hours to produce one unit of Y. The company's objective function equation would be: a) $15X + $12Y = $60; b) $15X + $12Y \le 60; c) Z = $15X + $12Y; d) none of these.

_____ 8. (Appendix) Refer to the data in question 7 above. The company's constraint equation for production time would be: a) 4X + 7Y \le 60; b) 4X + 7Y = 60; c) Z = 4X + 7Y; d) none of these.

Complete the Statements

Fill in the necessary words to complete the following statements.

1. All costs are relevant in decision making except those costs which are not _____

2. Depreciation on equipment which has already been purchased is a _____ cost.

3. If by dropping a product line a company is not able to avoid as much in _____ as it loses in contribution margin, then the product line should be retained.

4. One of the great dangers in allocating _____ fixed costs is that such allocations can make a product line look less profitable than it really is.

5. A decision to produce a fabricated part internally, rather than to buy the part externally from a supplier, is often called a _____ decision.

6. If a company is involved in more than one of the steps from the extraction of raw materials to the completion of a final product, it is said to be _____ _____

7. One of the key considerations in a make or buy decision is the _____ cost of the space being used to make a part rather than to buy it.

8. Total contribution margin will be maximized by promoting those products or accepting those orders that promise the highest contribution margin in relation to the _____ resources of the firm.

9. Two or more products that are produced from a common input are known as _____ products.

10. The _____-_____ point is that point in the manufacturing process at which the joint products can be recognized as individual units of output.

11. (Appendix) In linear programming, the _____ _____ represents the goal that is to be achieved. This goal could be either to maximize total contribution margin or to minimize total cost.

12. (Appendix) A key step in a linear programming solution is to recognize the _____ under which a firm must operate, and express them in equation form.

13. (Appendix) The solution to a linear programming problem is found in the _____ _____, which is bounded by the lines formed by the constraint equations.

Exercises

13-1. The most recent income statement for Department C of Merrill's Department Store is given below:

Sales		$500,000
Less variable expenses		200,000
Contribution margin		300,000
Less fixed expenses:		
Salaries and wages	$150,000	
Insurance on inventories	10,000	
Depreciation of equipment	65,000	
Advertising	100,000	325,000
Net income (loss)		$(25,000)

Management is thinking about dropping the department, due to its poor showing. If the department is dropped, one employee will be retained. Her salary is $30,000. The equipment has no resale value. Prepare an analysis to determine whether or not the department should be dropped:

Contribution margin lost if the
  department is dropped $

Less fixed costs which can
  be avoided if the department is
  dropped:

_____ $

_____

_____   _____   _____

Increase (decrease) in overall
  company net income $

Based on the analysis above, Department C (should/should not) _____ be dropped.

Redo the analysis, using the alternate format shown below:

	Keep Department C	Drop Department C	Difference: Net income increase or (decrease)
Sales	$500,000	$	$
Less variable expenses	200,000		
Contribution margin	300,000		
Less fixed expenses:			
Salaries and wages	150,000		
Insurance on inventories	10,000		
Depreciation of equipment	65,000		
Advertising	100,000		
Total fixed expenses	$325,000		
Net income (loss)	$(25,000)	$	$

13-2. Watson Company produces two products from a common input. Data relating to the two products are given below:

	Product A	Product B
Sales value at the split-off point	$60,000	$120,000
Allocated joint product costs	45,000	90,000
Sales value after further processing	90,000	200,000
Cost of further processing	20,000	85,000

Determine which of the products should be sold at the split-off point, and which should be processed further before sale.

Sales value after further processing	$	$
Sales value at the split-off point	_____	_____
Incremental revenue from further processing		
Less cost of further processing	_____	_____
Profit (loss) from further processing	$	$

13-3. Petre Company is now producing a small part that is used in the production of one of its product lines. The company's accounting department reports the following costs of producing the part internally:

	Per Part
Direct materials	$15
Direct labor	10
Variable overhead	2
Fixed overhead, direct	4
Fixed overhead, common, but allocated	5
Total cost	$36

The direct fixed overhead costs consist of 75 percent depreciation of special equipment, and 25 percent supervisory salaries. The special equipment has no resale value.

An outside supplier has offered to sell the parts to Petre Company for $30 each, based on an order of 5,000 parts per year. Determine whether Petre Company should accept this offer, or continue to make the parts internally:

	Per Unit Differential Costs		5,000 Parts	
	Make	Buy	Make	Buy
Outside purchase price				
Cost of making internally:				
Total cost	$	$	$	$
Difference in favor of (making/buying) _____		$		$

13-4. (Appendix) Monson Company manufactures two products, A and B. The company operates under three constraints: the weight of the products, the amount of raw materials available, and the amount of available production capacity. A graphical analysis of these three constraints is given below:

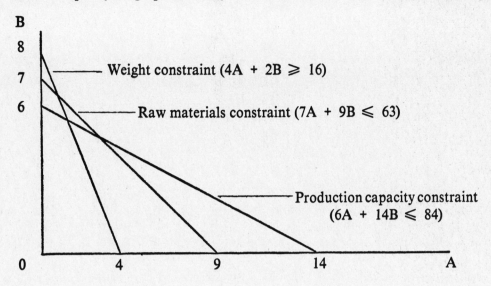

Shade the feasible production area on the above graph. Be careful to watch the direction of the constraint!

13-5. (Appendix) H-P Company manufactures two products, H and P. It takes four hours to manufacture H and two hours to manufacture P. The company operates three eight-hour shifts. H requires one pound of raw material per unit and P requires three pounds per unit. The supplier of raw material will provide only 30 pounds of raw material per day. Upon completion, H weighs 16 ounces, and P weighs 2½ pounds. The combination of products shipped to customers should weigh at least 10 pounds. H has a contribution margin of $4.50 per unit, and P has a contribution margin of $8 per unit.

    a.   What is the objective function equation?

    b.   Determine the constraint equations for:
        (1)   Time constraint:

        (2)   Raw material constraint:

        (3)   Shipping constraint:

Chapter 13
Answers to Questions and Exercises

True or False

1.	T	7.	T	13.	T
2.	F	8.	T	14.	T
3.	F	9.	F	15.	T
4.	T	10.	F	16.	F
5.	F	11.	T	17.	T
6.	T	12.	F	18.	T

Multiple Choice

1. b
2. c
3. d
4. d
5. b
6. b
7. c
8. a

Complete the Statements

1. avoidable
2. sunk
3. fixed cost
4. common
5. make or buy
6. vertically integrated
7. opportunity
8. scarce
9. joint
10. split-off
11. objective function
12. constraints
13. feasible production area

Exercises

13-1.

Contribution margin lost if the department is dropped		$300,000
Less fixed costs which can be avoided if the department is dropped:		
Salaries and wages ($150,000 − $30,000)	$120,000	
Insurance on inventories	10,000	
Advertising	100,000	230,000
Decrease in overall company net income		$ (70,000)

Based on the analysis above, Department C should not be dropped. Solution using the alternate format:

	Keep Department C	Drop Department C	Difference: Net income increase or (decrease)
Sales	$500,000	$ -0-	$(500,000)
Less variable expenses	200,000	-0-	200,000
Contribution margin	300,000	-0-	$(300,000)
Less fixed expenses:			
Salaries and wages	150,000	30,000	120,000
Insurance on inventories	10,000	-0-	10,000
Depreciation of equipment	65,000	65,000	-0-
Advertising	100,000	-0-	100,000
Total fixed expenses	325,000	95,000	230,000
Net income (loss)	$(25,000)	$(95,000)	$ (70,000)

13-2.

	Product A	Product B
Sales value after further processing	$ 90,000	$200,000
Sales value at the split-off point	60,000	120,000
Incremental revenue from further processing	30,000	80,000
Less cost of further processing	20,000	85,000
Profit (loss) from further processing	$ 10,000	$ (5,000)

13-3.

	Per Unit Differential Costs		5,000 Parts	
	Make	Buy	Make	Buy
Outside purchase price		$30		$150,000
Cost of making internally:				
Direct materials	$15		$ 75,000	
Direct labor	10		50,000	
Variable overhead	2		10,000	
Fixed overhead, direct	1*		5,000	
Fixed overhead, common, but allocated	--		--	
Total cost	$28	$30	$140,000	$150,000
Difference in favor of making	$2		$10,000	

*$4 × 25% = $1. The depreciation on the equipment, and the common fixed overhead would not be avoidable costs.

13-4.

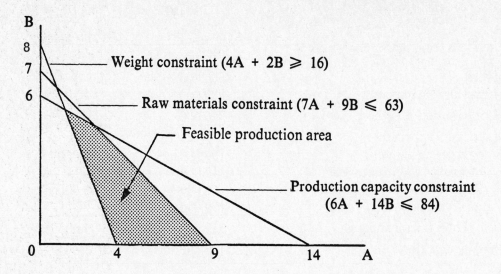

Remember that the direction of a constraint is *inward* if the equation is expressed in terms of less than or equal to ($\leqslant$), whereas the direction of the constraint is *outward* if the equation is expressed in terms of greater than or equal to ($\geqslant$).

13-5.   a. $Z = 4.50H + 8P$

b.   (1)   Time constraint: $4H + 2P \leqslant 24$
        (2)   Raw material constraint: $H + 3P \leqslant 30$
        (3)   Shipping constraint: $H + 2.5P \geqslant 10$

Chapter 14

Capital Budgeting Decisions

Chapter Study Suggestions

In order to understand the material in this chapter, you must have a solid understanding of the concept of present value. If you have not worked with present value before, study the section early in the chapter titled, "The Theory of Interest," until you thoroughly understand what present value is and how it is computed. Then turn to Exercise 14-1 and work it through. The solution to this exercise is given immediately following the exercise itself.

Once you understand present value, you will be ready to tackle the capital budgeting methods illustrated in the chapter. The first of these methods is called the net present value method. This method is illustrated in Exhibits 14-3 and 14-6. Follow through each number in the exhibits, and trace the factors back into the tables given at the end of the chapter. Unless you do this, you won't really understand what is going on. Also note the format in which the data are presented. You should use a similar format in your own homework problems.

The second method presented for capital budgeting is called the time-adjusted rate of return method. It is illustrated in Example D and Exhibit 14-7. This method is very different from the net present value method, so spend an equal amount of time studying how it is computed.

Finally, at the end of the chapter the net present value method is expanded in Exhibits 14-9 through 14-12. Once you have gone through these exhibits step-by-step you should have a good understanding of the material in the chapter.

CHAPTER HIGHLIGHTS AND STUDY GUIDE

A. The term capital budgeting is used to describe those actions relating to the planning and financing of capital outlays, such as for the purchase of new equipment, for the introduction of new product lines, and for the modernization of plant facilities. Capital budgeting is an investment concept, since it involves a commitment of funds now in order to receive some desired return in the future.

    1. Typical capital budgeting decisions encountered by the business executive are:

        a. Cost reduction decisions.
        b. Plant expansion decisions.
        c. Equipment selection decisions.
        d. Equipment replacement decisions.

    2. Capital budgeting decisions fall into two broad categories:

    a. Screening decisions: Those decisions relating to whether or not a proposed project meets some preset standard of acceptance.

    b. Preference decisions: Those decisions relating to the selection of a proposed project from among several *competing* courses of action.

    3. Business investments have two key characteristics that must be recognized in a study of capital budgeting methods.

    a. The first characteristic is that most business investments involve depreciable assets. The return provided by such investments must be sufficient to do two things: (1) provide a return *on* the original investment; and (2) return the total amount of the original investment itself.

    b. The second characteristic is that the returns on most business investments extend over long periods of time.

    4. Since most business investments extend over long periods of time, it is important to recognize the time value of money in capital budgeting analysis. Essentially, the time value of money says that a dollar received today is more valuable than a dollar received in the future. There are two reasons why a dollar received today is more valuable:

    a. The first reason is that the dollar received today can be invested and earn an immediate return.

    b. The second reason is that there is uncertainty about the future, and therefore a dollar in the future may never be received.

    5. Present value analysis makes it possible for the manager to recognize the time value of money in capital budgeting decisions.

    a. Present value analysis involves the expressing of a future cash flow in terms of present dollars. When a future cash flow is expressed in terms of its present value, the process is called *discounting*.

    b. To determine the present value of a single sum to be received in the future, Table 3 in Appendix B to the chapter should be used. This table contains factors for various rates of interest for various periods, which, when multiplied by the future sum, will give the sum's present value.

    c. To determine the present value of an *annuity*, or stream, of cash flows, Table 4 in Appendix B to the chapter should be used. This table contains factors which, when multiplied by the stream of cash flows, will give the stream's present value.

B. Because business investments tend to be long-term in nature, a business should pay particular attention to the time value of money in investment decisions. The discounted cash flow methods give full recognition to the time value of money, and at the same time provide for full recovery of original capital. There are two discountd cash flow methods available—net present value, and time-adjusted rate of return.

C. The net present value method is illustrated in Example A (Exhibit 14-3) and in Example C (Exhibit 14-6). The basic steps in this method are:

    1. Determine the required investment.

    2. Determine the future cash inflows or outflows associated with the investment.

    3. Use the appropriate present value tables to determine the present value of the future cash flows.

4. Subtract the initial investment from the present value of the future cash flows. This difference is called the *net present value.*

5. If the net present value determined from step (4) is zero or positive, the investment should be accepted. If the net present value is negative, the investment should be rejected. To summarize, note the following example:

	Case 1	Case 2	Case 3
Initial investment (outflow)	$(5,000)	$(4,500)	$(5,200)
Present value of future cash inflows	5,000	5,000	5,000
Net Present Value	$ -0-	$ 500	$ (200)
Decision	Accept	Accept	Reject

D. The emphasis of discounted cash flow analysis is on *cash flows*—not on accounting net income. Accounting net income must be ignored in cash flow analysis, since accounting net income does not take into account the timing of cash flows into and out of an organization.

1. Typical cash flows associated with an investment are:

    a. Cash Outflows: Initial investment (including installation costs).
    Increased working capital needs.
    Repairs and maintenance.
    Incremental operating costs.

    b. Cash Inflows: Incremental revenues.
    Reductions in costs.
    Salvage value.
    Release of working capital.

2. Depreciation is not considered in capital budgeting analysis. There are two reasons why it is not considered:

    a. Depreciation is an accounting concept not involving a current cash outflow. As indicated above, in capital budgeting the emphasis is on cash flows.

    b. Discounted cash flow methods automatically provide for return of the original investment, thereby making a depreciation deduction unnecessary. This is illustrated in Exhibits 14-4 and 14-5.

3. There are two limiting assumptions in discounted cash flow analysis. These are:

    a. All cash flows occur at the *end* of a period.

    b. All cash flows generated by an investment project are immediately reinvested in another project which yields a rate of return at least as large as the first project.

E. The time-adjusted rate of return (or internal rate of return) is another discounted cash flow method used in capital budgeting decisions.

1. The time-adjusted rate of return can be defined as the true interest yield promised by an investment project over its useful life.

2. The time-adjusted rate of return can be computed by finding that discount rate which will equate the present value of the investments (cash outflows) required by a project with the present value of the returns (cash inflows) that the project promises.

3. The formula for computing the time-adjusted rate of return is:

$$\frac{\text{Investment}}{\text{Annual cash flows}} = \text{Factor of the time-adjusted rate of return.}$$

For example, assume an investment of $3,791 is made in a project which will last five years and has no salvage value. Also assume that the annual cash inflow from the project will be $1,000.

$$\frac{\$3,791}{\$1,000} = \text{Factor of the time-adjusted rate of return for a 5-year annuity.}$$

$$3.791 = \text{Factor of the time-adjusted rate of return for a 5-year annuity.}$$

From Table 4 in Appendix B, scanning along the 5-year row, it can be seen that this factor represents a 10 percent rate of return.

4. If the cash flows are uneven, *a trial and error approach* must be used to find the time-adjusted rate of return.

5. Interpolation is a process used if the factor for the time-adjusted rate of return falls between two factors from the present value tables. The interpolation process is illustrated in the chapter.

6. The time-adjusted rate of return can be compared against the required rate of return (usually the cost of capital) a company has selected for investment projects. If the time-adjusted rate of return is less than the cost of capital, the project is rejected. If it is greater than or equal to the cost of capital, the project is accepted.

F.   The cost of capital is a screening tool to help managers screen out undesirable investment projects. The cost of capital is a broad concept involving a blending of the cost of *all* sources of capital funds, both debt and equity.

1. Under the time-adjusted rate of return method, the cost of capital is the *hurdle* rate which the project must clear for acceptance.

2. Under the net present value method, the cost of capital becomes the *actual discount rate* used to compute the net present value of a proposed project.

G.   The net present value method has a number of advantages over the time-adjusted rate of return method.

1. The net present value method is easier to use.

2. The net present value method makes it easier to adjust for risk.

3. The net present value method provides more usable information.

H.   Two common approaches used in the net present value method are the *total-cost* approach and the *incremental* cost approach.

1. The total-cost approach is the most flexible and the most widely used method.

a. Follow through Exhibit 14-9 to see how this approach is used.

b. Note in Exhibit 14-9 that *all* cash inflows and *all* cash outflows are included in the solution under each alternative.

2. The incremental cost approach is a simpler and more direct route to a decision. This approach focuses on differential costs. Follow through Exhibit 14-10 which shows this approach.

3. The final net present value figure that serves as a criteria for the decision is the *same* under the total-cost approach or incremental approach.

J.   Sometimes no revenue or cash inflow is directly involved in a decision. In this situation, the company will select the *least-cost* project. The least-cost can be determined by either the total-cost approach or the incremental approach. Least-cost decisions are illustrated in Exhibits 14-11 and 14-12.

APPENDIX: Inflation and Capital Budgeting

A.   Inflation has an impact on the numbers which are used in a capital budgeting analysis, but it does not have an impact on the *results* which are obtained.

B.   Refer to the data in Exhibit 14-13. In "Solution B" inflation is given full consideration. Note the following points about Solution B:

1. Annual cash inflows are adjusted for the effects of inflation by multiplying each year's cash inflow by a price-index number which reflects the current inflation rate. (Note from the exhibit how the index number is computed.)

2. The cost of capital is adjusted for the effects of inflation by adding together three cost elements.

a. These elements are (1) the cost of capital, (2) the inflation rate, and (3) a combined factor which allows for the reinvestment of inflation-generated earnings.

b. For example, if the cost of capital is 15 percent and the inflation rate is 8 percent, then the inflation-adjusted cost of capital would be:

Cost of capital	15.0%
Inflation rate	8.0
Combined effect (15% × 8%)	1.2
Inflation-adjusted cost of capital	24.2%

c. A frequent error in adjusting data for inflation is to omit part or all of the computations in "b" above.

3. If the computations in "2" are properly made, then the same net present value will be obtained in a capital budgeting analysis as if no adjustments had been made.

a. The reason the same net present value is obtained is that in adjusting the data for the effects of inflation we adjust *both* the cash flows and the discount rate, and thus the inflationary effects cancel themselves out.

B. In actual practice, not all companies make adjustments for inflation when doing a capital budgeting analysis.

　　1. The reasons no adjustments are made are: 1) the computations are very complex, and 2) the same net present value can be obtained using unadjusted data.

2. If no adjustments are made for inflation when the original capital budgeting analysis is made, then some adjustments should be made in the post-audit to ensure that both estimated and actual data are comparable. This can be accomplished by either adjusting the estimated data for the *actual* inflation which has taken place, or by adjusting the actual data downward to remove any inflationary element.

REVIEW AND SELF TEST
Questions and Exercises

True or False

For each of the following statements, enter a T or an F in the blank to indicate whether the statement is true or false.

_____ 1. The commitment of funds by a business into inventory, equipment, and like assets is an investment, the same as a purchase of stocks or bonds by an individual.

_____ 2. The reason why a manager would prefer to receive a dollar today than to receive a dollar a year from now is that money has a time value.

_____ 3. The process of computing the present value of a future sum is called compounding.

_____ 4. Present value and future value are just two ways of expressing a given sum.

_____ 5. Under the net present value method, the present value of all cash inflows associated with an investment project are compared against the present value of all cash outflows, with the difference, or net present value, determining whether or not the project is an acceptable investment.

_____ 6. If the net present value of an investment project is zero, then the project should be rejected since it is not providing any return on the investment involved.

_____ 7. One key shortcoming of discounted cash flow methods is that they ignore the recovery of original investment.

_____ 8. Although depreciation is an important element in the computation of accounting net income, it is not considered in capital budgeting computations, since it does not involve a cash flow.

_____ 9. Although a cash outlay for a noncurrent asset such as a machine would be considered in a capital budgeting analysis, a cash outlay for a working capital item such as inventory would not be considered.

_____ 10. Cost of capital is a broad concept, involving a blending of the costs of all sources of capital, both debt and equity.

_____ 11. In discounted cash flow analysis, cash flows are assumed to occur uniformly throughout a period.

_____ 12. The time-adjusted rate of return is that discount factor which will cause a project's net present value to be zero.

_____ 13. If the cash flows of a project are uneven, then the project's time-adjusted rate of return can't be computed.

_____ 14. Depreciation is an example of an out-of-pocket cost.

_____ 15. To be acceptable, a project's time-adjusted rate of return can't be less than the company's cost of capital.

_____ 16. The time-adjusted rate of return method is simpler to use, makes it easier for the manager to adjust for risk, and provides more usable information than the net present value method.

Multiple Choice

Choose the best answer or response by placing the identifying letter in the space provided.

_____ 1. A key characteristic of business investments is that they: a) involve depreciable assets; b) are fairly short-term in nature; c) involve nondepreciable assets; d) none of these.

_____ 2. The process of determining the present value of a future sum is called: a) compounding; b) interpolating; c) discounting; d) none of these.

_____ 3. Out-of-pocket costs would include: a) all costs shown on the income statement; b) actual cash outlays made during the period for salaries, advertising, and like operating expenses; c) depreciation on any item which has already been purchased; d) none of these.

_____ 4. Acme Company is considering investing in a new machine which costs $8,688, and which has a useful life of 8 years with no salvage value. The machine will generate $2,000 annually in net cash inflows. The time-adjusted rate of return on the machine is: a) 14 percent; b) 16 percent; c) 18 percent; d) 20 percent; e) none of these.

The following data relate to questions 5 and 6.

Peters Company is considering the purchase of a machine to further automate its production line. The machine would cost $30,000, and have a ten-year life with no salvage value. It would save $8,000 per year in labor costs, but would increase power costs by $1,000 annually. The cost of capital is 12 percent.

_____ 5. The present value of the net annual cost savings would be: a) $39,550; b) $45,200; c) $5,650; d) none of these.

_____ 6. The net present value of the proposed machine would be: A) $(15,200); b) $5,650; c) $9,550; d) none of these.

Complete the Statements

Fill in the necessary words to complete the following statements.

1. Capital budgeting decisions tend to fall into two broad categories—_____ decisions and _____ decisions.

2. In order to have data available for decision-making purposes, the manager will often discount future sums to their _____ _____

3. A series, or stream, of cash flows is known as an _____

4. The _____ _____ _____ of an investment project is determined by deducting the present value of its cash inflows from the present value of its cash outflows.

5. The _____-_____ rate of return can be defined as the true interest yield of an investment project over its useful life.

6. In computing the net present value of a project, a company generally will use its_____ _____ _____ as the discount rate.

7. In addition to the cost of new equipment, when a firm undertakes a new project it often will have to make an investment in _____ _____, which includes amounts expended for added inventory, accounts receivable, and like assets.

8. The cost of capital acts as a _____ tool, helping the manager to cull out undesirable investment projects.

9. Decisions in which revenues are not directly involved are called _____-_____decisions.

10. When interest is paid on interest, the process is called _____ of interest.

Exercises

14-1. You have recently won $100,000 in a contest. You have been given the option of receiving $100,000 today or receiving $12,000 at the end of each year for the next 20 years.

Which of these two options would you select if you can invest money at:

a.   8 percent.

Item	Year(s) Having Cash Flows	Amount of Cash Flows	8 Percent Factor	Present Value of Cash Flows
Receive the annuity		$		$
Receive the lump-sum				_____
Net present value in favor of the _____				$ _____

b.   12 percent.

Item	Year(s) Having Cash Flows	Amount of Cash Flows	12 Percent Factor	Present Value of Cash Flows
Receive the annuity		$		$
Receive the lump-sum				_____
Net present value in favor of the _____				$ _____

14-2. Lynde Company has been offered a contract to provide a key part for the U.S. Army. The contract would expire in eight years. The projected cash flows that would be associated with the contract are given below:

Cost of new equipment	$300,000
Working capital needed	100,000
Net annual cash receipts from the Army	85,000
Salvage value of the equipment in eight years	50,000

The company's cost of capital is 16 percent. Complete the analysis below to determine whether or not the contract should be accepted.

Item	Year(s) Having Cash Flows	Amount of Cash Flows	16 Percent Factor	Present Value of Cash Flows
Cost of new equipment		$		$
Working capital needed				
Net annual cash receipts				
Salvage value of equipment				
Working capital released				_____
Net present value				$ _____

Should the contracted by accepted? Explain.

_____

_____

_____

_____

14-3. Swift Company wants to purchase a new machine which will cost $20,000. The machine will provide revenues of $9,000 per year. Out-of-pocket operating costs will be $6,000 per year. The new machine will have a useful life of 10 years. The company's cost of capital is 12 percent.

a.   What is the time-adjusted rate of return? (Interpolate if necessary.)

Annual revenue . . . . $ _____

Annual operating costs . . . . _____

  Net annual cash inflow . . . . _____

$$\frac{\text{Initial investment}}{\text{Net annual cash inflow}} = \text{Factor of the time-adjusted rate of return}$$

_____ =

_____ *Present Value Factor*

_____ percent factor . . . .

True factor . . . .

_____ percent factor . . . . _____   _____

Difference . . . . ======   ======

TAROR = _____ percent + (——————— × 2%) =

b.   Should the company buy the new machine? Why or why not?

_____

_____

_____

_____

_____

_____

_____

Chapter 14
Answers to Questions and Exercises

True or False

1.	T	7.	F	12.	T
2.	T	8.	T	13.	F
3.	F	9.	F	14.	F
4.	T	10.	T	15.	T
5.	T	11.	F	16.	F
6.	F				

Multiple Choice

1. a
2. c
3. b
4. b
5. a
6. c

Complete the Statements

1.	preference, screening	6.	cost of capital
2.	present value	7.	working capital
3.	annuity	8.	screening
4.	net present value	9.	least-cost
5.	time-adjusted	10.	compounding

Exercises

14-1. a. You would prefer to receive the annuity:

Item	Year(s) Having Cash Flows	Amount of Cash Flows	8 Percent Factor	Present Value of Cash Flows
Receive the annuity	1-20	$ 12,000	9.818	$117,816
Receive the lump-sum	Now	100,000	1.000	100,000
Net Present Value in Favor of the Annuity				$ 17,816

b. You would prefer to receive the lump-sum:

Item	Year(s) Having Cash Flows	Amount of Cash Flows	12 Percent Factor	Present Value of Cash Flows
Receive the annuity	1-20	$ 12,000	7.469	$ 89,628
Receive the lump-sum	Now	100,000	1.000	100,000
Net Present Value in favor of the Lump-Sum				$ 10,372

14-2.

Item	Year(s) Having Cash Flows	Amount of Cash Flows	16 Percent Factor	Present Value of Cash Flows
Cost of new equipment	Now	($300,000)	1.000	($300,000)
Working capital needed	Now	(100,000)	1.000	(100,000)
Net annual cash receipts	1-8	85,000	4.344	369,240
Salvage value of equipment	8	50,000	0.305	15,250
Working capital released	8	100,000	0.305	30,500
Net present value				$ 14,990

Yes, the contract should be accepted. The net present value is positive, which means that the contract will provide more than the company's 16 percent required rate of return.

14-3. a.

Annual revenue	$9,000
Annual operating costs	6,000
Incremental Cash Inflow	$3,000

$$\frac{\text{Initial Investment}}{\text{Annual Cash Inflow}} = \text{Factor of the time-adjusted rate of return}$$

$$\frac{\$20,000}{\$ 3,000} = 6.667.$$

Since the 6.667 factor falls between the 8 percent and 10 percent rates of return in Table 4, it will be necessary to interpolate to find the exact rate of return:

	Present Value Factor	
8 percent factor	6.710	6.710
True rate	6.667	
10 percent factor		6.145
Difference	.043	.565

$$\text{Time-adjusted rate of return} = 8 \text{ percent} + \left(\frac{.043}{.565} \times 2 \text{ percent} \right)$$

Time-adjusted rate of return = 8.15 percent.

b. No, reject the machine since the 8.15 percent time-adjusted rate of return is less than the 12 percent cost of capital.

Chapter 15

Further Aspects of Investment Decisions

Chapter Study Suggestions

This chapter builds on the discounted cash flow methods introduced in Chapter 14 and discusses the impact of income taxes on capital budgeting decisions. The formulas showing the computation of after-tax cost and after-tax benefit should be committed to memory. In addition, the formula for the tax shield associated with depreciation should be memorized. Exhibit 15-6 shows a comprehensive illustration of the computation of net present value when income tax factors are considered. Study this exhibit and the related text material with special care; the computations on the exhibit are complex and will take some time to digest.

Two methods are illustrated in the chapter for ranking investment projects according to preference. These are: 1) the time-adjusted rate of return method, and 2) the profitability index. Notice that the profitability index is based on the net present value concepts discussed in the preceding chapter. It is tricky to compute, so follow the text example through step-by-step.

At the end of the chapter, two methods of making capital budgeting decisions are illustrated that do not utilize discounted cash flows. These are: 1) the payback method, and 2) the simple rate of return method. Formulas are provided for both methods that should be committed to memory. Pay particular attention to the formula for the simple rate of return. It is deceptively difficult and can be tricky to apply in a problem situation.

145

CHAPTER HIGHLIGHTS AND STUDY GUIDE

A. Income taxes have an effect on the cash flows of profit-making entities and therefore must be considered in discounted cash flow methods of capital budgeting. Nonprofit entities such as hospitals, schools, or governmental units are not subject to income taxes and will always use the approaches illustrated in Chapter 14.

B. Since expenses are tax-deductible in most companies, managers generally look at their expenses on an after-tax basis, rather than on a before-tax basis.

   1. The true cost of a tax-deductible item is not the dollars paid out, but the amount of the payment that will remain after taking into account any reduction in income taxes that the payment will bring about.

   2. An expenditure net of its tax effects is known as *after-tax cost*. For example, assume that a company needs to overhaul a machine at a cost of $6,000. The overhaul is tax-deductible. If the income tax rate is 40 percent, the after-tax cost is:

Cost of overhaul	$6,000
Reduction in taxes due to the overhaul	
(40 percent × $6,000)	(2,400)
After-Tax Cost	$3,600

   3. The concept of after-tax cost is very useful to the manager, since it measures the *actual* amount of cash that will be leaving a company as a result of a particular expenditure decision.

   4. The formula that will give the after-tax cost of *any* tax-deductible expenditures is:

(1 − Tax rate) × Cash expense = After-tax cost

C. In capital budgeting decisions, revenues must also be placed on an after-tax basis.

   1. The cash inflow from revenues in a company should not be measured by the actual dollars received, but by the amount that will remain after taking into consideration any additional income taxes that the revenues will bring about.

   2. A receipt net of its tax effect is known as *after-tax benefit*. For example, assume that a company receives revenue of $100,000, in cash. The income tax rate is 40 percent. The after-tax benefit is:

Revenue	$100,000
Income tax payment required	
(40 percent × $100,000)	(40,000)
After-Tax Benefit	$ 60,000

   3. If a company has a savings in cost by using machine A instead of machine B, the savings are treated the same as a revenue item in determining the net after-tax cash inflow.

   4. Not all cash receipts are taxable. For example, the release of working capital at the termination of an investment project is not a taxable cash inflow.

   5. The formula that will give the after-tax cash inflow from revenue or other *taxable* cash receipts is:

$$\begin{pmatrix} 1 - \text{Tax} \\ \text{rate} \end{pmatrix} \times \begin{matrix} \text{Cash} \\ \text{receipt} \end{matrix} = \begin{matrix} \text{After-tax benefit} \\ \text{(net cash inflow)} \end{matrix}$$

D. Depreciation deductions in and of themselves do not involve cash flows. However, because the depreciation deduction does have an effect on the amount of taxes that a firm will pay, it does have an effect on the cash outflow paid for taxes.

   1. The depreciation deduction acts as a *shield* against tax payments. In effect, depreciation deductions *shield* revenues from taxation and thereby *lower* the amount of income taxes that a company has to pay.

   2. The formula used to compute the depreciation tax shield is:

$$\begin{matrix} \text{Depreciation} \\ \text{deduction} \end{matrix} \times \begin{matrix} \text{Tax} \\ \text{rate} \end{matrix} = \begin{matrix} \text{Tax savings from the} \\ \text{depreciation tax shield} \end{matrix}$$

E. For tax purposes, companies must use the Accelerated Cost Recovery System (ACRS) to depreciate assets. ACRS should also be used to compute depreciation for capital budgeting purposes.

   1. Under ACRS, assets are placed into one of five property classes, which provide for rapid acceleration of depreciation deductions. An optional straight-line method can be elected in lieu of the acceleration.

   2. In addition to depreciation, companies can also take what is known as an investment credit. In computing the investment credit, companies can choose one of two options.

a. The first option is to take a 10 percent investment credit on assets in the 5-year property class and a 6 percent investment credit on assets in the 3-year property class. If this option is chosen, then the depreciable cost of the asset must be reduced by one-half of the investment credit taken.

b. The second option is to take only an 8 percent investment credit on assets in the 5-year property class and a 4 percent investment credit on assets in the 3-year property class. Under this option, the entire cost of the asset can be depreciated.

F.   A comprehensive example of income taxes and capital budgeting is given in Exhibit 15-6. The reader should turn to this example and follow it through step by step.

1. Notice that all cash flows involving tax deductible expenses and taxable receipts have been placed on an after-tax basis by multiplying the cash flow in each case by one minus the tax rate.

2. Notice that the depreciation deductions have to be multiplied *by the tax rate itself* to determine the tax savings (cash inflow) resulting from the tax shield. *These two points should be studied with great care until both are thoroughly understood.*

G.   Preference decisions involve the ranking of investment projects.

1. Because investment funds are usually limited, a company needs some means of selecting among investment projects that compete for those funds.

2. Preference decisions are sometimes called *ranking* decisions or *rationing* decisions because they attempt to ration limited investment funds among competing investment opportunities.

3. When using the time-adjusted rate of return to rank competing investment projects, the preference rule is: *The higher the time-adjusted rate of return, the more desirable the project.*

4. If the net present value method is being used to rank competing investment projects, the net present value of one project can't be compared directly to the net present value of another project, unless the investments in the projects are of equal size.

a. To make a valid comparison between projects, a *profitability index* must be computed. The formula for the profitability index is:

$$\frac{\text{Present value of cash inflows}}{\text{Investment required}} = \frac{\text{Profitability}}{\text{index}}$$

b. The preference rule using the profitability index is: *The higher the profitability index, the more desirable the project.*

5. The profitability index is conceptually superior to the time-adjusted rate of return as a method of making preference decisions because the profitability index will always give the correct signal as to the relative desirability of alternatives, even if alternatives have different lives and different patterns of earnings.

H.   There are other methods to aid in capital budgeting decisions that do not involve discounted cash flow. One of these is the payback method.

1. The payback method computes the time period that is required for an investment project to recoup its own initial cost out of the cash receipts which it generates. The payback period is expressed in years. The formula is:

$$\frac{\text{Payback}}{\text{Period}} = \frac{\text{Investment Required}}{\text{Net Annual Cash Inflow}}$$

a. In computing the "Investment Required," if new equipment is replacing old equipment, then the cost of the new equipment should be reduced by any salvage value obtained from the old equipment.

b. In computing the "Net Annual Cash Inflow," if new equipment is replacing old equipment, then only the *incremental* cash inflow provided by the new equipment over the old equipment should be used.

2. The payback method is not a measure of profitability. Rather it is a measure of how long it takes for a project to recoup its own investment cost.

3. Major defects in the payback method are that it ignores the time value of money, and that it does not discriminate between projects of different useful lives.

I.   Another capital budgeting method that does not involve discounted cash flow is the simple rate of return method.

1. The simple rate of return method focuses on accounting net income, rather than on cash flows. The formula for its computation is:

$$\text{Simple rate of return} = \frac{[\text{Incremental revenue}] - \text{Operating expenses (including depreciation)}}{\text{Initial investment}}$$

or

$$\text{Simple rate of return} = \frac{\text{Incremental net income}}{\text{Initial investment}}$$

2. If the project is a cost reduction project, the formula becomes:

$$\text{Simple rate of return} = \frac{\text{Reduction in costs} - \text{Depreciation}}{\text{Initial investment}}$$

If new equipment is replacing old equipment, then the "Initial Investment" in the new equipment is the cost of the new equipment reduced by any salvage value obtained from the old equipment.

3. A major defect of the simple rate of return method is that it does not consider the time value of money. Therefore, the rate of return computed by this method will not be an accurate guide as to the profitability of an investment project.

APPENDIX: Income tax effects on payback and simple rate of return

A. The formula for computing the payback period when taxes are considered is the same as used earlier in the chapter, except that the data must be adjusted for the investment credit. The formula is:

$$\text{Payback period} = \frac{\text{Investment required} - \text{Investment credit}}{\text{Net annual cash inflow}}$$

B. For the simple rate of return, the formula to be used when income taxes are considered is:

Simple rate of return =

$$\frac{\text{Incremental revenues} - \text{Incremental expenses, including depreciation and income taxes} = \text{Net income}}{\text{Initial investment} - \text{Investment credit}}$$

Or, if the project is a cost reduction project, the formula becomes:

$$\text{Simple rate of return} = \frac{\text{Reduction in costs} - \text{Depreciation and taxes}}{\text{Initial investment} - \text{Investment credit}}$$

REVIEW AND SELF TEST
Questions and Exercises

True or False

For each of the following statements, enter a T or an F in the blank to indicate whether the statement is true or false.

_____ 1. Tax-deductible expenses of a business are often looked at on an after-tax basis, rather than on a before-tax basis.

_____ 2. The after-tax cost of a tax-deductible item is computed by the formula: Tax rate × Cash expense = After-tax cost.

_____ 3. If a company takes an 8 percent investment credit on an asset in the 5-year property class, the credit reduces the amount of depreciation which can be taken on the asset for tax purposes.

_____ 4. If a company's depreciation deduction is $50,000 and its tax rate is 40 percent, then the tax savings from the depreciation tax shield is: $(1 - .40) \times \$50,000 = \$30,000$.

_____ 5. There is no tax benefit if a company incurs a loss in replacing one piece of equipment with another.

_____ 6. When using the time-adjusted rate of return method to rank competing investment projects, the preference rule is: The higher the time-adjusted rate of return, the more desirable the project.

_____ 7. When using the net present value method to rank competing investment projects, the preference rule is: The higher the net present value, the more desirable the project.

_____ 8. The profitability index is computed by dividing the present value of the cash inflows associated with a project by the present value of the investment required.

_____ 9. The profitability index is conceptually superior to the time-adjusted rate of return as a method of making preference decisions.

_____ 10. The payback period can be defined as the length of time that it takes for an investment project to recoup its own initial cost out of the net cash receipts it generates.

_____ 11. The basic premise of the payback method is that the longer the payback period, the more desirable is the investment.

_____ 12. In using the payback method, if new equipment is replacing old equipment, then any salvage received on disposal of the old equipment should be deducted from the cost of the new equipment, and only the incremental investment used in the payback computation.

_____ 13. The payback method can't be used if cash inflows are uneven from year to year.

_____ 14. One defect of the simple rate of return method is that it does not consider the time value of money.

_____ 15. The simple rate of return method and the time-adjusted rate of return method will generally yield the same rate of return figure.

_____ 16. The payback method and the simple rate of return method are both inferior to the discounted cash flow methods of making capital budgeting decisions.

Multiple Choice

Choose the best answer or response by placing the identifying letter in the space provided.

_____ 1. The accounting net income figure is used by which of the following capital budgeting methods: a) net present value; b) time-adjusted rate of return; c) payback; d) simple rate of return; e) none of these.

_____ 2. The Accelerated Cost Recovery System: a) requires that all assets be depreciated over a 5-year period; b) ignores the concept of useful life; c) requires that salvage value be considered on all assets; d) can be used only on depreciable real property; e) none of these.

_____ 3. Project A requires an investment of $40,000, has a present value of cash inflows of $50,000, and a net present value of $10,000. The project's profitability index would be: a) 1.25; b) 4.0; c) 0.80; d) none of these.

_____ 4. Frumer Company wants to purchase a machine that costs $21,000. The following annual revenues and expenses would be associated with the new machine:

Sales		$40,000
Less operating expenses:		
Salaries, rent, etc.	$33,000	
Depreciation	2,000	35,000
Net income		$ 5,000

The payback period on the new machine would be (ignore income taxes): a) 8 years; b) 3 years, c) 4 years; d) none of these.

_____ 5. The simple rate of return method: a) is conceptually superior to the net present value method; b) will generally yield the same rate of return as the time-adjusted rate of return method; c) does not consider the time value of money; d) none of these.

_____ 6. Roland Company has purchased a piece of equipment for use in its research and development program. This equipment: a) must be depreciated by the optional straight-line method; b) falls in the ACRS 3-year property class; c) does not qualify for the investment credit; d) none of these.

_____ 7. (Appendix) Machine X costs $50,000. It falls in the ACRS 5-year property class. If the company that purchases machine X elects to use the 8 percent investment credit, then the "Investment" figure to be used in a payback computation would be: a) $46,000; b) $50,000; c) $54,000; d) none of these.

Complete the Statements

Fill in the necessary words to complete the following statements.

1. An expenditure net of its tax effect is known as _____-_____ cost.

2. A decision as to which of two otherwise acceptable projects should be selected is called a _____ decision.

3. When using the time-adjusted rate of return method to rank competing investment projects, the preference rule is: The _____ the time-adjusted rate of return, the more desirable the project.

4. Preference decisions are sometimes called _____ decisions, since they attempt to ration limited investment funds among many competing investment opportunities.

5. The _____ index is used to make preference decisions between investment projects, when the net present value method has been used for screening purposes.

6. The _____ period can be defined as the length of time that it takes for an investment project to recoup its own initial cost out of the cash receipts which it generates.

7. If new equipment is replacing old equipment, then any salvage received on disposal of the old equipment should be deducted from the cost of the new equipment, and only the _____ investment used in a payback computation.

8. The payback period is computed by dividing a project's initial investment by its net annual _____ _____.

9. The simple rate of return is computed by dividing a project's _____ _____, as shown on the income statement, by the project's initial investment.

10. The most damaging criticism of the simple rate of return method is that it does not consider the _____ _____ of money.

Exercises

15-1. Martin Company is acquiring a new machine for use on its production line. The following data relate to the new machine:

Cost of the new machine	$80,000
Annual savings in cash operating costs	30,000
Salvage value of the new machine	6,000
Overhaul of the new machine required in the third year	4,000
Life of the new machine	4 years

The new machine is replacing an old machine that is fully depreciated, but which has a remaining book value of $18,000. The old machine can be sold now for $12,000.

Assume that the company's tax rate is 40 percent.

a. Compute the after-tax savings in annual cash operating costs. $_____

b.   Compute the after-tax cost of the overhaul required in the third year. $_____

c.   Compute the tax savings from the depreciation tax shield. You may assume that the company uses the ACRS tables and that the machine falls in the 3-year property class. The company ignores salvage value in computing depreciation deductions.

Year	Cost	ACRS Percentage	Depreciation Deduction	Tax Rate	Tax Shield: Income Tax Savings
1	$80,000			40%	
2					
3					

d.   Compute the after-tax benefit from the salvage value of the new machine. $_____

e.   Compute the after-tax cash inflow from sale of the old machine. (This is a tough one, and you may have to refer to the computations in Exhibit 15-7 in the text.)

Cash received from the sale $ _____

Tax savings from loss on sale:
    Current book value $ _____
    Sale price now   _____
    Loss on disposal
    Multiply by the tax rate   × 40%
    Tax savings from loss $ _____

15-2. Marvel Company has $50,000 to invest and is considering two alternatives:

	Investment X	Investment Y
Cost of equipment	$50,000	—
Working capital needed	—	$50,000
Annual cash inflows	20,000	20,000
Life of the project	5 years	5 years

The company's cost of capital is 12 percent, and the tax rate is 40 percent.

a.   Compute the net present value of each investment. The company uses straight-line depreciation on all equipment. The equipment falls in the ACRS 3-year property class.

Item	Year(s)	Amount of Cash Flow	12% Factor	Present Value of Cash Flows
Investment X:				
Cost of equipment		$		$
Investment credit				
Annual cash inflows				

Depreciation:

Year	Dep'n. Deduction	Tax Rate	Tax Savings
1			
2			
3			
4			

Net present value $ _____

Item	Year(s)	Amount of Cash Flow	12% Factor	Present Value of Cash Flows
Investment Y:				
Working capital needed		$		$
Annual cash inflows				
Working capital released				
Net present value				$

b. Compute the profitability index for each investment, and explain which investment should be chosen.

$$\frac{\text{Present Value of Cash Inflows}}{\text{Investment Required}} = \text{Profitability Index}$$

Investment X: Investment Y:

_____ =   _____ =

_____

_____

_____

15-3. Hardee Company would like to purchase a new machine which dispenses yogurt. The machine costs $450,000. Annual revenues and expenses which would be associated with the new yogurt machine follow:

Sales revenue		$300,000
Less operating expenses:		
Advertising	$100,000	
Salaries of operators	70,000	
Maintenance	30,000	
Depreciation	40,000	
Total expenses		240,000
Net income		$ 60,000

a. Hardee Company will not invest in new equipment unless it promises a payback period of 4 years or less. Compute the payback period on the yogurt machine. Ignore income taxes.

Computation of the net annual cash inflow:

Net income	$
Add: Noncash deduction for depreciation	
Net annual cash inflow	$

Computation of the payback period:

$$\frac{\text{Investment required}}{\text{Net annual cash inflow}} = \text{Payback period}$$

$$\underline{\hspace{4cm}} = \qquad \text{years}$$

Should the machine be purchased? Explain. _____

_____

_____

b.   Assume that Hardee requires a 16 percent return on all equipment purchases. Compute the simple rate of return promised by the new machine. Ignore income taxes.

$$\frac{\overset{\text{Incremental}}{\underset{\text{revenue}}{}} - \overset{\text{Operating}}{\underset{\text{expenses}}{}} = \overset{\text{Net}}{\underset{\text{income}}{}}}{\text{Initial investment}} = \text{Simple rate of return}$$

$$\underline{\hspace{4cm}} = \qquad \%$$

Should the machine be purchased? Explain. _____

_____

_____

15-4. (Appendix) Recreation Outlets, Inc., is considering the purchase of a water slide for one of its amusement parks. The slide would cost $200,000 installed and have a 10-year useful life. The following revenues and expenses would be associated with the slide:

Admission fees		$176,000
Operating expenses:		
Salaries	$35,000	
Maintenance	20,000	
Insurance	7,000	
Depreciation	40,000	
Utilities	18,000	
Total expenses		120,000
Taxable income		56,000
Less income tax(40%)		22,400
Net income		$ 33,600

The slide would fall in the ACRS 5-year property class. The company uses straight-line depreciation. (For simplicity, the half-year convention has been ignored in computing straight-line depreciation above.) The slide would quality for the investment credit.

a. Assume that the company requires a payback period of 5 years or less for all investments. Compute the payback period.

Computation of the net annual cash inflow:

Net income $ _____
Add: Noncash deduction for depreciation   _____
Net annual cash inflow $ _____

Computation of the payback period:

$$\frac{\text{Investment required } - \text{ Investment credit}}{\text{Net annual cash flow}} = \text{Payback period}$$

$$\frac{\rule{7cm}{0.4pt}}{} = \quad \text{years.}$$

Should the waterslide be purchased? Explain. _____

_____

_____

b. Assume that the company's after-tax cost of capital is 14 percent. Compute the simple rate of return on the waterslide.

$$\frac{\text{Incremental revenues } - \begin{array}{c}\text{Incremental expenses,}\\ \text{including depreciation}\\ \text{and income taxes}\end{array} = \text{Net income}}{\text{Initial investment } - \text{ Investment credit}} = \begin{array}{c}\text{Simple rate}\\ \text{of return}\end{array}$$

$$\frac{\rule{7cm}{0.4pt}}{} = \quad \%.$$

Should the waterslide be purchased? Explain. _____

_____

_____

Chapter 15
Answers to Questions and Exercises

True or False

1.	T	9.	T
2.	F	10.	T
3.	F	11.	F
4.	F	12.	T
5.	F	13.	F
6.	T	14.	T
7.	F	15.	F
8.	T	16.	T

Multiple Choice

1. d
2. b
3. a
4. b
5. c
6. b
7. a

Complete the Statements

1.	after-tax	6.	payback
2.	preference	7.	incremental
3.	higher	8.	cash inflows
4.	rationing or ranking	9.	net income
5.	profitability	10.	time value

Exercises

15-1. a.   (1 − Tax Rate) × Total Amount Received = After-Tax Benefit
   (1 − .40) × $30,000 = $18,000

b.   (1 − Tax Rate) × Total Amount Paid = After-Tax Cost
   (1 − .40) × $4,000 = $2,400

c.   The tax shield from depreciation is:

Depreciation Deduction × Tax Rate = Tax Savings from Depreciation Tax Shield

Year	Cost	ACRS Percentage	Depreciation Deduction	Tax Rate	Tax Shield: Income Tax Savings
	(1)	(2)	(1) × (2) = (3)	(4)	(3) × (4)
1	$80,000	25%	$20,000	40%	$ 8,000
2	$80,000	38%	30,400	40%	12,160
3	$80,000	37%	29,600	40%	11,840

d. (1 − Tax Rate) × Total Amount Received = After-Tax Benefit
    (1 − .40) × $6,000 = $3,600

e. Cash flow from disposal of the old machine:

Cash received from sale	$12,000
Tax savings from loss on sale:	
Current book value	$18,000
Sale price now	12,000
Loss on disposal	6,000
Multiply by the tax rate	× 40%
Tax savings from loss	$ 2,400

15-2. a.

Item		Year(s)	Amount of Cash Flow	12% Factor	Present Value of Cash Flows
Investment X:					
Cost of equipment		Now	($50,000)	1.000	($50,000)
Investment credit	(4% × $50,000)	1	2,000	0.893	1,786
Annual cash inflows	$20,000				
Multiply by 1 − 40%	× 60%				
After-tax cash inflow	$12,000	1-5	12,000	3.605	43,260

Depreciation:

Year	Dep'n Deduction	Tax Rate	Tax Savings				
1	$ 8,333	40%	$3,333	1	3,333	0.893	2,976
2	16,667	40%	6,667	2	6,667	0.797	5,314
3	16,667	40%	6,667	3	6,667	0.712	4,747
4	8,333	40%	3,333	4	3,333	0.636	2,120
Net present value							$10,203

Item		Year(s)	Amount of Cash Flow	12% Factor	Present Value of Cash Flows
Investment Y:					
Working capital needed		Now	($50,000)	1.000	($50,000)
Annual cash inflows	$20,000				
Multiply by 1 − 40%	× 60%				
After-tax cash inflow	$12,000	1-5	12,000	3.605	43,260
Working capital released		5	50,000	0.567	28,350
Net present value					$21,610

b. Investment X: Investment Y:

$$\frac{\$60,203}{\$50,000} = 1.20 \text{ (rounded)} \qquad \frac{\$71,610}{\$50,000} = 1.43 \text{ (rounded)}$$

Investment Y should be chosen, since its profitability index is higher than Investment X's profitability index.

15-3. a.   The net annual cash inflow would be:

Net income	$ 60,000
Add: Noncash deduction for depreciation	40,000
Net annual cash inflow	$100,000

The payback period would be:

$$\frac{\$450,000}{\$100,000} = 4.5 \text{ years.}$$

The machine should not be purchased since it will not provide the 4 year payback period required by the company.

b.   The simple rate of return would be:

$$\frac{\$60,000}{\$450,000} = 13.3\%.$$

The machine should not be purchased since the simple rate of return which it promises (13.3%) is less than the 16 percent return required by the company.

15-4. a.   Computation of the net annual cash inflow:

Net income	$33,600
Add: Noncash deduction for depreciation	40,000
Net annual cash inflow	$73,600

Computation of the payback period:

$$\frac{\$200,000 - \$16,000^* = \$184,000}{\$73,600} = 2.5 \text{ years.}$$

*$200,000 \times 8\% = \$16,000.$

Yes, the waterslide should be purchased. It provides a payback of less than the 5-year maximum set by the company.

b. $$\frac{\$33,600}{\$200,000 - \$16,000 = \$184,000} = 18.3\% \text{ (rounded).}$$

Yes, the waterslide should be purchased. The 18.3 percent simple rate of return which it promises is greater than the company's 14 percent after-tax cost of capital.

Chapter 16

Service Department Cost Allocations

Chapter Study Suggestions

There are three key exhibits in this chapter—Exhibits 16-5, 16-6, and 16-7. Exhibits 16-5 and 16-6 illustrate the step method and the direct method of allocating service department costs to producing departments. Follow the computations in the exhibits through step-by-step, and note the difference in the way the two exhibits handle the cost data.

Exhibit 16-7 expands on Exhibits 16-5 and 16-6 by showing how costs can be broken down into their variable and fixed components, and thus can be allocated by behavior. Spend the bulk of your study time on the sections titled, "Allocating costs by behavior," and "Guidelines for allocating service department costs." Then note from Exhibit 16-7 how the ideas in these two sections are implemented in an actual allocation problem. This is a very important exhibit, since it is the basis for many of the longer, more difficult homework problems.

CHAPTER HIGHLIGHTS AND STUDY GUIDE

A. The two broad classes of departments within a firm are: 1) producing departments, and 2) service departments. A department which works directly on the product of the organization is a producing department, whereas a service department provides service or assistance that facilitates the activities of producing departments.

B. The costs of service departments must be allocated to producing departments. These allocated costs are then added to the overhead costs of the producing departments, and included in the computation of predetermined overhead rates.

1. This allocation process is illustrated in Exhibits 16-1 and 16-2. Study these exhibits carefully to get an overview of the allocation of service department costs to producing departments.

2. There are four broad areas which must be considered in deciding how to make an equitable allocation of service department costs to producing departments. These four areas are discussed in sections C, D, E, and F below.

C. Care must be taken to select an allocation base which reflects as accurately as possible the benefits to be received by the various producing departments from the services involved.

1. Criteria for selecting an allocation base may include:

    a. Direct, traceable benefits from the service involved.
    b. The extent of facilities provided.
    c. The ease of making an allocation.

2. Selection of an allocation base represents *a major policy decision* that is reviewed only at very infrequent intervals, or when it appears that some major inequity exists.

D. Service departments not only provide service to producing departments, but also to each other. Services provided by one service department to another are called *inter-departmental services*. A cafeteria for all company employees, including service department employees, is an example of an inter-departmental service.

1. There are two approaches to handling the allocation of inter-departmental service costs: 1) the step method, and 2) the direct method.

2. The *step method* provides for the allocation of a department's costs to other service departments, as well as to producing departments, in a sequential manner.

    a. The sequence of allocation typically begins with the department which provides the greatest amount of service to other departments.

    b. Exhibits 16-4 and 16-5 provide graphical and numerical examples of the step method.

    c. Once a service department's costs have been allocated out, no costs are subsequently reallocated back to it.

    d. The service department costs allocated to producing departments are added in with the producing departments' own overhead costs, for purposes of computing predetermined overhead rates in the producing departments.

3. The *direct method* ignores the costs of services between service departments, and allocates all service department costs directly to producing departments. The direct method is illustrated in Exhibit 16-6.

    a. Because the direct method ignores inter-departmental services, it is less accurate than the step method.

    b. When a cost allocation is not accurate, it distorts the predetermined overhead rates which, in turn, can lead to ineffective pricing.

    c. The direct method is widely used in practice, however, because of its ease of application.

E. Whenever possible, service department costs should be separated into fixed and variable classifications and allocated separately. By allocating fixed and variable costs separately, a company can avoid possible inequities in allocation as well as provide data which is useful for planning and controlling operations.

1. Variable costs represent direct costs of providing services, and will generally vary in total proportionately with fluctuations in the level of service consumed.

    a. As a general rule, variable costs should be charged to consuming departments according to whatever activity base controls the incurrence of the cost involved.

b. The assigning of variable service costs to consuming departments can more accurately be termed "charges" than allocations.

2. The fixed costs of service departments represent the cost of having long-run service capacity available. These costs are most equitably allocated to consuming departments on the basis of *predetermined, lump-sum amounts.*

a. The lump-sum amount may be based either on long-run average servicing needs, or on peak-period servicing needs of other departments.

b. Once set, lump-sum allocations of fixed costs will not vary from period to period.

F.   Some pitfalls to avoid in allocating fixed costs are:

1. A company should not allocate fixed costs by the use of a *variable* allocation base. An inequity will arise since fixed costs allocated to one department will be influenced heavily by what happens in other departments.

2. A company should not allocate actual service department costs to producing departments, but instead should allocated *budgeted* costs. The allocation of actual costs passes on the inefficiencies in operations by service department managers to producing department managers.

3. Any variance over budgeted costs should be retained in the service department and closed out against cost of goods sold, along with producing department variances.

G.   Five guidelines for allocating service department costs are:

1. If possible, the distinction between variable and fixed costs should be maintained.

2. Variable costs should be allocated at the budgeted rate, according to whatever activity measure controls the incurrence of the cost involved.

3. Fixed costs should be allocated in predetermined, lump-sum amounts.

4. If it is not feasible to maintain a distinction between variable and fixed costs in a service department, the costs of the department should be allocated to consuming departments according to that base which appears to provide the best measure of benefits received.

5. Where feasible, reciprocal services between departments should be recognized.

H.   For product costing purposes, the general rule is that *all* service department costs which are incurred as a result of specific services provided to producing departments should be allocated back to these departments and added to product costs via the predetermined overhead rate. This rule is not to be followed if it is felt by management that doing so would produce an undesirable response from producing departments.

1. Sometimes service department services are provided free in order to facilitate their acceptance by producing departments.

2. Instead of services being provided free, a fixed retainer fee is sometimes charged to the producing departments. This is done to encourage the producing departments to use the services involved up to the specified level for which the retainer fee has been paid.

I.   Sales dollars are sometimes used as an allocation base.

1. One reason for using sales dollars is that the sales dollar figure is simple and easy to work with. Another reason is that managers tend to view sales dollars as a measure of well-being, or "ability to pay."

2. However, since sales dollars represent a variable allocation base, inequities can result if fixed costs are being allocated.

3. Sales dollars should be used as an allocation base only in those cases where there is a direct causal relationship between sales dollars and the service department costs being allocated.

REVIEW AND SELF TEST
Questions and Exercises

True or False

For each of the following statements, enter a T or an F in the blank to indicate whether the statement is true or false.

_____ 1. Service departments are often engaged directly in the production process.

_____ 2. Service department costs should be included as part of the cost of a company's products, the same as materials, labor, and overhead.

_____ 3. The predetermined overhead rates used in producing departments should include allocated costs from service departments.

_____ 4. As costs are allocated from service departments to producing departments, these costs should be included on the producing departments' flexible budgets.

_____ 5. Allocation bases used to allocate service department costs should be changed as frequently as possible.

_____ 6. If a service department (such as a cafeteria) generates revenues, these revenues should not be considered in allocating the service department's costs to producing departments.

_____ 7. In allocating costs by the step method, the allocation sequence typically begins with the service department which provides the greatest amount of service to other departments.

_____ 8. Under the step method of cost allocation, costs are allocated both backward and forward.

_____ 9. The direct method of cost allocation is much simpler than the step method, in that services provided between service departments are ignored.

_____ 10. Variable costs of service departments should be allocated to producing departments in predetermined, lump-sum amounts.

_____ 11. If a variable allocation base (such as direct labor hours) is used to allocate fixed service department costs, inequities may result in the amount of cost allocated to the various producing departments.

_____ 12. Budgeted costs, rather than actual costs, should always be allocated from service departments to producing departments.

_____ 13. Sales dollars constitute the best allocation base that the manager can use.

_____ 14. Under the retainer fee approach, producing departments are charged only for the amount of services which they actually consume.

Multiple Choice

Choose the best answer or response by placing the identifying letter in the space provided.

_____ 1. Allocation bases used to allocate service department costs to producing departments: a) are not used for purposes of computing predetermined overhead rates; b) remain unchanged for long periods of time, once they are chosen; c) have a heavy influence on the amount of cost ultimately charged to a unit of product; d) responses a, b, and c are all correct; e) none of these.

The following information applies to multiple choice questions 2-6.

The budgeted and peak-period machine hours of Wasatch Company's two producing departments follow:

| | Machine Hours | |
	Budgeted	Peak-Period
Production Department #1	15,000	20,000
Production Department #2	25,000	30,000
Total Machine Hours	40,000	50,000

The Wasatch Company has a repair department which services these two producing departments. The variable servicing costs are budgeted at $.20 per machine hour. Fixed costs are budgeted at $12,000 per year. Fixed service costs are allocated to producing departments on the basis of peak-period machine hours.

At the end of the year, the actual machine hours worked by the producing departments were 16,000 hours for Department #1 and 24,000 hours for Department #2. The actual repair department costs were: variable costs—$8,600, and fixed costs—$13,000.

____ 2. The budgeted variable costs allocated to Department #1 at the beginning of the year will be: a) $3,000; b) $5,000; c) $4,800; d) $7,200; e) none of the above.

____ 3. The lump-sum budgeted fixed costs allocated to Department #2 at the beginning of the year will be: a) $3,000; b) $5,000; c) $4,800; d) $7,200; e) none of the above.

____ 4. The actual variable costs allocated to Department #1 at the end of the year will be: a) $4,800; b) $5,200; c) $3,200; d) $7,200; e) none of the above.

____ 5. The actual fixed costs allocated to Department #2 at the end of the year will be: a) $4,800; b) $7,800; c) $3,200; d) $7,200; e) none of the above.

____ 6. The total spending variance for fixed and variable costs of the repair department at the end of the year will be: a) $600; b) $1,600; c) $1,000; d) $1,400; e) none of the above.

Complete the Statements

Fill in the necessary words to complete the following statements.

1. A department which does not work directly on products, but which provides assistance to other departments is known as a _____ department.

2. One allocation method, known as the _____ method, provides for allocation of a service department's costs to other service departments, as well as to producing departments, in a sequential manner.

3. Another allocation method, known as the _____ method, ignores the cost of services between departments, and allocates all service department costs directly to producing departments.

4. Technically, the assigning of variable service department costs to consuming departments can be more accurately termed "_____" than allocations, since the service department is charging the consuming department at some fixed rate per unit of service provided.

5. Fixed costs of service departments should be allocated to consuming departments in predetermined _____-_____ amounts.

6. A _____ allocation base should never be used to allocate fixed costs from service departments to producing departments.

7. A service department should always allocate _____ costs, rather than actual costs, to other departments.

8. Under the _____ fee approach for assigning service department costs to producing departments, each department is charged a flat amount each year, regardless of how much or how little of the service it utilizes.

Exercises

16-1. Piney Company has three service departments and two producing departments. Following are costs and other data relating to these departments:

	Service Departments			Production Departments	
	Janitorial	*Cafeteria*	*Engineering*	*Assembly*	*Finishing*
Overhead costs before allocation	$60,000	$42,600	$75,000	$250,000	$300,000
Square feet	1,500 sq. ft.	2,000 sq. ft.	1,000 sq. ft.	4,000 sq. ft.	3,000 sq. ft.
Number of employees	15	12	50	200	400

The Janitorial department performs the greatest amount of service to the other departments, followed by the Cafeteria, with the Engineering department last. Allocate Janitorial costs on the basis of square feet. The Cafeteria and Engineering costs should be allocated on the basis of the number of employees. The company makes no distinction between variable and fixed service department costs.

Allocate service department costs to the producing departments using the step method.

	Service Departments			Production Departments	
	Janitorial	*Cafeteria*	*Engineering*	*Assembly*	*Finishing*
Overhead costs before allocation					
Allocation:					
Janitorial					
Cafeteria					
Engineering					
Total Overhead Costs After Allocation					

16-2. Refer to the data in Exercise 16-1. Allocate service department costs to the producing departments using the direct method.

	Service Departments			Production Departments	
	Janitorial	*Cafeteria*	*Engineering*	*Assembly*	*Finishing*
Overhead costs before allocation					
Allocation:					
Janitorial					
Cafeteria					
Engineering					
Total Overhead Costs After Allocation					

Chapter 16
Answers to Questions and Exercises

True or False

1.	F	8.	F
2.	T	9.	T
3.	T	10.	F
4.	T	11.	T
5.	F	12.	T
6.	F	13.	F
7.	T	14.	F

Multiple Choice

1. d
2. a
3. d
4. c
5. d
6. b

Complete the Statements

1.	service	5.	lump-sum
2.	step	6.	variable
3.	direct	7.	budgeted
4.	charges	8.	retainer

Exercises

16-1.

	Service Departments			Production Departments	
	Janitorial	Cafeteria	Engineering	Assembly	Finishing
Overhead costs before allocation	$60,000	$42,600	$75,000	$250,000	$300,000
Allocation:					
Janitorial[1]	(60,000)	12,000	6,000	24,000	18,000
Cafeteria[2]...........		(54,600)	4,200	16,800	33,600
Engineering[3]			(85,200)	28,400	56,800
Total Overhead Costs After Allocation	-0-	-0-	-0-	$319,200	$408,400

1. $\dfrac{\text{Janitorial Cost}}{\text{Total Square Feet}} = \dfrac{\$60,000}{10,000 \text{ sq. ft.}} = \$6/\text{sq. ft.}$

2. $\dfrac{\text{Cafeteria Cost}}{\text{Number of Employees}} = \dfrac{\$54,600}{650} = \$84/\text{employee}$

3. $\dfrac{\text{Engineering Cost}}{\text{Number of Employees}} = \dfrac{\$85,200}{600} = \$142/\text{employee}$

16-2.

	Service Departments			Production Departments	
	Janitorial	*Cafeteria*	*Engineering*	*Assembly*	*Finishing*
Overhead costs before allocation	$60,000	$42,600	$75,000	$250,000	$300,000
Allocation:					
Janitorial[1]	(60,000)			34,286	25,714
Cafeteria[2]		(42,600)		14,200	28,400
Engineering[3]			(75,000)	25,000	50,000
Total Overhead Costs After Allocation	-0-	-0-	-0-	$323,486	$404,114

1. $$\frac{\text{Janitorial Cost}}{\text{Total Square Feet}} = \frac{\$60,000}{7,000 \text{ sq. ft.}} = \$8.57/\text{sq. ft. (rounded)}$$

2. $$\frac{\text{Cafeteria Cost}}{\text{Number of Employees}} = \frac{\$42,600}{600} = \$71/\text{employee}$$

3. $$\frac{\text{Engineering Cost}}{\text{Number of Employees}} = \frac{\$75,000}{600} = \$125/\text{employee}$$

Chapter 17

"How Well Am I Doing?"— Financial Statement Analysis

Chapter Study Suggestions

The chapter is divided into two parts. The first part discusses the preparation and use of statements in comparative and common-size form. Your study time in this part should be focused on Exhibits 17-1 through 17-4. These exhibits show how statements in comparative and common-size form are prepared and used by the manager to assess the well-being of the firm.

The second part of the chapter deals with ratio analysis. Altogether, some seventeen ratios are presented in this part of the chapter. In your study, you should memorize the formula for each ratio since you will be expected to know these formulas on quizzes and examinations. You should also learn how to interpret each ratio. A summary of the ratios is given in Exhibit 17-7 to aid you in your study.

CHAPTER HIGHLIGHTS AND STUDY GUIDE

A. The purpose of financial statement analysis is to assist statement users in predicting the future course of events in an organization.

    1. All users of financial data—stockholders, creditors, and management—have concerns that can be resolved to some degree by the predictive ability of statement analysis.

    2. To be most useful for predictive purposes, the results of any financial statement analysis should be in comparative form.

        a. This comparison should be against other periods, as well as against other firms within the industry.

        b. Unfortunately, comparisons between firms are often made difficult by differences in accounting methods in use.

    3. The analyst must be careful not to rely just on ratios and other analytical tools in making a judgment about a firm.

        a. Rather than an end, ratios should be viewed as being a starting point, and as being indicators of what to pursue in greater depth.

        b. The analyst must also look at industry trends, technological changes, changes in consumer tastes, and so forth, in judging the probable future of a firm.

B. Three common analytical techniques for financial statement analysis are: 1) dollar and percentage changes on statements; 2) common-size statements; and 3) ratios.

    1. Dollar and percentage changes on statements are determined through a technique known as *horizontal analysis*. Horizontal analysis involves the placing of two or more statements side by side and analyzing the changes between years.

        a. Showing changes in dollar form identifies key factors affecting profitability or financial position.

        b. Showing changes in percentage form helps the analyst to gain perspective, and to gain a feel for the significance of the changes that have taken place.

        c. Horizontal analysis can also be done by computing *trend percentages*. Trend percentages state several years' financial statements in terms of a base year.

    2. A common-size statement is one that shows the separate items on it in percentage form, rather than in dollar form. Preparation of common-size statements is known as *vertical analysis.*

        a. Showing the balance sheet and the income statement in common-size form helps the manager to see the relative importance of the various assets, and also to see the relative importance of the various expense items in relation to sales.

        b. Common-size statements are also very helpful in pointing out efficiencies and inefficiencies that otherwise might go unnoticed.

    3. In addition to the above analytical techniques, ratios can be prepared to assist stockholders, short-term creditors, and long-term creditors in assessing the well-being of a firm. Ratios which are designed to meet the needs of these three different groups are discussed in sections C, D, and E following.

C. The common stockholder wants to measure his or her well-being. There are several ratios which act as indicators of shareholder well-being.

    1. *Earnings per share* is an important measure of the annual earnings remaining for common shareholders. The formula is:

$$\frac{\text{Net income} - \text{Preferred dividends}}{\text{Common shares outstanding}} = \text{Earnings per share}$$

        a. If a company has extraordinary gains or losses appearing as part of net income, the company must show two earnings per share figures. First, earnings per share must be shown for *normal* operations; and second, the effect on earnings per share must be shown for *extraordinary items.*

        b. By showing the effect of extraordinary items on earnings per share, the distorting influence of the extraordinary items on net income is highlighted. In addition, the trend of normal earnings can be evaluated by the analyst.

        c. When reporting extraordinary items separately, they must be shown "net of their tax effect."

        d. If a company has convertible securities, the earnings per share figure must again be computed in two ways. First, it must be computed assuming no conversion of the convertible securities into common stock; and second, it must be computed assuming full conversion of the convertible securities into common stock. The latter computation is referred to as earnings per share computed on a *fully diluted* basis.

2. The *price-earnings ratio* is a measure used to gauge stock values. It shows the relationship between the market price of a share of stock and the stock's current earnings per share. The price-earnings ratio is computed by the following formula:

$$\frac{\text{Market price}}{\text{Earnings per share}} = \text{Price/earnings ratio}$$

3. The *dividend payout ratio* gauges the portion of current earnings being paid out as dividends. The formula is:

$$\frac{\text{Dividends per share}}{\text{Earnings per share}} = \text{Dividend payout ratio}$$

4. The *dividend yield ratio* provides the investor with a measure of the opportunity cost of his or her investment in terms of yield. The ratio is computed by the following formula:

$$\frac{\text{Dividends per share}}{\text{Market price per share}} = \text{Dividend yield ratio}$$

5. The *return on total assets* ratio is a measure of how well assets have been employed by a firm. It is a measure of *operating performance*. The formula is:

$$\frac{\text{Net Income} + \left[\begin{array}{c}\text{Interest expense} \times \\ (1 - \text{tax rate})\end{array}\right]}{\text{Average total assets}} = \text{Return on total assets}$$

a. Notice that the interest expense is placed on an after-tax basis before being added back to net income.

b. The reason for adding the interest expense back to net income is to derive a net income figure that shows earnings *before* any distributions have been made to either creditors or stockholders. Thus we eliminate the matter of how the assets were financed from influencing the measurement of how well the assets have been employed.

6. The *return on common stockholders' equity* is a measure of a company's ability to generate income for the benefit of common stockholders. The formula is:

$$\frac{\text{Net income less preferred dividends}}{\begin{array}{c}\text{Average common stockholders' equity} \\ \text{(average total stockholders' equity less} \\ \text{preferred stock)}\end{array}} = \begin{array}{c}\text{Return on} \\ \text{common} \\ \text{stockhold-} \\ \text{ers' equity}\end{array}$$

a. The return on common stockholders' equity is usually higher than the return on total assets because of financial leverage (sometimes called "trading on the equity").

b. Financial leverage involves the financing of assets in a company with funds that have been acquired from creditors or from preferred stockholders at a fixed rate of return. If the assets in which the funds are invested earn a greater return than the fixed rate of return required by the suppliers of the funds, then financial leverage is *positive*. Leverage is *negative* if the assets earn a return which is less than the fixed rate required by the suppliers of the funds.

c. Leverage sources include long-term debt, preferred stock, and current liabilities.

d. Since interest on long-term debt is tax-deductible, it is a more effective source of positive leverage than is preferred stock.

e. The leverage principle amply illustrates that prudent use of debt in the capital structure can substantially benefit the common stockholder.

7. The *book value per share* measures the net assets per share of common stock. The formula is:

$$\frac{\begin{array}{c}\text{Common stockholders' equity (Total} \\ \text{stockholders' equity} - \text{Preferred stock)}\end{array}}{\text{Number of common shares outstanding}} = \begin{array}{c}\text{Book} \\ \text{value} \\ \text{per share}\end{array}$$

a. A book value per share that is less than the market value per share is not an indication that the stock is overpriced. Market value is geared toward future earnings and dividends; by contrast, book value is geared toward the past, in that it reflects the results of already completed transactions.

b. Book value is of limited usefulness to the manager, since it is geared to the past rather than to the future.

D. The short-term creditor is concerned with the near-term prospects of having obligations paid on time. As such, he or she is more interested in cash flows and in working capital management than in how much accounting net income is being reported by a company.

1. *Working capital* is a measure of the assets financed from long-term capital sources that do not require near-term payment. Working capital is computed by the following formula:

Current assets − Current liabilities = Working capital

2. The *current ratio* is a widely used measure of short-term debt-paying ability. The formula is:

$$\frac{\text{Current assets}}{\text{Current liabilities}} = \text{Current ratio}$$

a. Although widely regarded as a measure of debt-paying ability, the current ratio must be interpreted with a great deal of care. The manager must look at the *composition* of the assets and liabilities that go into the computation of the ratio, rather than just looking at their total amount.

b. The general rule of thumb calls for a current ratio of 2 to 1. However, this general rule is subject to many exceptions, depending on the industry and firm involved.

3. The *acid-test or quick ratio* is designed to measure how well a company can meet its short-term obligations using only its *most liquid* current assets. The formula is:

$$\frac{\text{Cash + Marketable securities +}}{\text{Current liabilities}} = \text{Acid-test ratio}$$

4. The *accounts receivable turnover* provides a rough gauge of how well accounts receivable are turning into cash. The formula is:

$$\frac{\text{Sales on account}}{\text{Average accounts receivable balance}} = \text{Accounts receivable turnover}$$

By dividing the turnover rate into 365 (the number of days in a year), the *average collection period* for accounts receivable can be computed.

5. The *inventory turnover* measures how many times a company's inventory has been sold during the year. The formula is:

$$\frac{\text{Cost of goods sold}}{\text{Average inventory balance}} = \text{Inventory turnover}$$

The number of days being taken to sell the entire inventory one time (called the *average sale period*) can be computed by dividing 365 by the inventory turnover figure.

E. The long-term creditor's position differs from that of the short-term creditor, since the long-term creditor is concerned with both the near-term and the long-term ability of a firm to meet its commitments.

1. The long-term creditor uses the *times interest earned ratio* to gauge the ability of a firm to meet its near-term commitments. The formula is:

$$\frac{\text{Earnings before interest expense and income taxes}}{\text{Interest expense}} = \text{Times interest earned}$$

Interest expense has a claim on earnings *before* any income taxes are paid. Therefore, earnings before income taxes is used in the computation above, rather than earnings after taxes.

2. The *debt-to-equity ratio* indicates the amount of assets being provided by creditors for each dollar of assets being provided by the owners of a company. The formula is:

$$\frac{\text{Total liabilities}}{\text{Stockholders' equity}} = \text{Debt-to-equity ratio}$$

Creditors would like the debt-to-equity ratio to be low, since that would mean that stockholders were providing most of the long-term financing for the company, thereby giving creditors a large cushion of protection.

REVIEW AND SELF TEST
Questions and Exercises

True or False

For each of the following statements, enter a T or an F in the blank to indicate whether the statement is true or false.

_____ 1. Although financial statement analysis is of considerable use to stockholders and creditors, it is of little use to management.

_____ 2. The results of financial statement analysis are of value only when viewed in comparison with the results of other periods or other firms.

_____ 3. Ratios are generally conclusive evidence as to whether or not a firm will be profitable in future years.

_____ 4. One purpose for placing financial statements in comparative form is to make it possible for the manager to study movements and trends in the data.

_____ 5. Trend percentages in financial statements would be an example of vertical analysis.

_____ 6. A common-size statement is one that shows the separate items appearing on it in percentage form, with each item stated as a percentage of some total of which that item is a part.

_____ 7. The earnings per share figure is computed *after* deducting preferred dividends from the net income of a company.

_____ 8. In computing the earnings per share figure, extraordinary gains and losses are simply lumped in with ordinary income and expense items.

_____ 9. If a company has convertible securities, then it should adjust its earnings per share figure to a fully diluted basis.

_____ 10. If earnings remain unchanged and the price/earnings ratio goes up, then one would expect the market price of a stock to go down.

_____ 11. Investors seeking capital gains would like the dividend payout ratio to be high.

_____ 12. In computing the dividend yield ratio, the investor should use the current market price for the stock, rather than the price which he or she paid for it.

_____ 13. In placing a before-tax item on an after-tax basis, the item should be multiplied by $1 -$ tax rate.

_____ 14. If the return on total assets is greater than the after-tax cost of long-term debt, then leverage is positive, and the common stockholders will benefit.

_____ 15. The inventory turnover is computed by dividing sales by average inventory.

Multiple Choice

Choose the best answer or response by placing the identifying letter in the space provided.

_____ 1. Placing several years' financial statements side-by-side and computing the change from year to year would be known as: a) vertical analysis; b) horizontal analysis; c) ratio analysis; d) none of these.

_____ 2. Long-term creditors would like the debt-to-equity ratio to be: a) low; b) high; c) equal to 1; d) none of these.

_____ 3. If the return on total assets is 10 percent, and if the return on common stockholders' equity is 12 percent, then: a) financial leverage is negative; b) the after-tax cost of long-term debt is probably greater than 10 percent; c) the after-tax cost of long-term debt is probably less than 10 percent; d) none of these.

_____ 4. The acid-test ratio: a) can be expected to be less than the current ratio; b) can be expected to be greater than the current ratio; c) could be either greater or less than the current ratio; d) none of these.

_____ 5. The payment of a current liability would cause the current ratio to: a) increase; b) decrease; c) remain unchanged; d) none of these.

_____ 6. An increase in the average collection period for accounts receivable would be explained by: a) an increase in the accounts receivable turnover ratio; b) a decrease in the average accounts receivable balance, with sales remaining unchanged; c) a tightening of credit policy in the company; d) none of these.

Complete the Statements

Fill in the necessary words to complete the following statements.

1. Preparation of common-size statements is known as _____ analysis.

2. The excess of current assets over current liabilities is known as _____ _____.

3. If a firm has convertible securities in its capital structure, then it should report its earnings per share on a fully _____ basis.

4. The dividend yield ratio is computed by dividing the dividends per share by the (market/original purchase) _____ price per share.

5. In order to place a before-tax item on an after-tax basis, the before-tax item should be multiplied by _____.

6. _____ _____ involves the securing of funds for investment at a fixed rate of return to the suppliers of the funds, normally with the thought in mind of enhancing the well-being of the common stockholders.

7. If the return to the common stockholders is greater than the return on total assets, then financial leverage is (positive/negative) _____.

8. The _____ _____ ratio measures how many times a company's inventory has been sold during the year.

9. The relationship between the market price of a share of stock and the stock's current earnings per share is often quoted in terms of a _____/ _____ ratio.

10. Trend percentages would be an example of (vertical/horizontal) _____ analysis of financial statements.

Exercises

17-1. The financial statements of Amfac, Inc., are given below:

AMFAC, INC.
Balance Sheet
December 31, 19x0

Assets

Cash	$ 8,000
Accounts receivable, net...	36,000
Merchandise inventory...	40,000
Prepaid expenses...	2,000
Plant and equipment, net..	214,000
Total Assets	$300,000

Equities

Current liabilities	$ 40,000
Long-term liabilities (10%)	60,000
Preferred stock (8%)...	50,000
Common stock, $10 par	30,000
Retained earnings	120,000
Total Equities	$300,000

AMFAC, INC.
Income Statement
For the Year Ended December 31, 19x0

Sales	$450,000
Cost of goods sold	270,000
Gross margin	$180,000
Operating expenses...	129,000
Net operating income	$ 51,000
Interest expense...	6,000
Net income before taxes..	$ 45,000
Income taxes (40%)...	18,000
Net Income	$ 27,000

Accounts receivable and inventory remained relatively constant during the year. There are no convertible securities. Assets at the beginning of the year totaled $250,000, and the stockholder's equity at the beginning of the year totaled $180,000. Preferred stock did not change during the year.

Compute the following:

a.   Current ratio.

b.   Acid-test ratio.

c. Debt-to-equity ratio.

d. Accounts receivable turnover in days.

e. Inventory turnover.

f. Times interest earned.

g Return on total assets.

h. Return on common stockholders' equity.

i. Is financial leverage positive or negative? Explain.

_____

_____

_____

17-2. Cartwright Company has reported the following data relating to sales and accounts receivable in its most recent annual report:

	19x5	19x4	19x3	19x2	19x1
Sales	$700,000	$675,000	$650,000	$575,000	$500,000
Accounts Receivable	$ 72,000	$ 60,000	$ 52,000	$ 46,000	$ 40,000

Express the data above in trend percentages. Use 19x1 as the base year.

	19x5	19x4	19x3	19x2	19x1
Sales	_____	_____	_____	_____	_____
Accounts Receivable	_____	_____	_____	_____	_____

Comment on the significant information revealed by your trend percentages:

_____

_____

_____

_____

17-3. Consider the following 19x1 and 19x2 income statements of Eldredge Company:

ELDREDGE COMPANY
Income Statements
For the Years Ended December 31, 19x1 and 19x2

	19x2	19x1
Sales	$600,000	$500,000
Cost of goods sold	420,000	331,000
Gross margin	$180,000	$169,000
Operating expenses:		
Selling expenses	$ 87,000	$ 72,500
Administrative expenses	46,800	51,000
Total operating expenses	$133,800	$123,500
Net operating income	$ 46,200	$ 45,500
Interest expense	1,200	1,500
Net income before taxes	$ 45,000	$ 44,000
Income taxes (40%)	18,000	17,600
Net Income	$ 27,000	$ 26,400

a. Express the income statements for both years in common-size percentages. Round percentages to one decimal point.

	19x2	19x1
Sales		
Cost of goods sold		
Gross margin	_____	_____
Operating expenses:		
Selling expenses		
Administrative expenses		
Total operating expenses	_____	_____
Net operating income		
Interest expense	_____	_____
Net income before taxes		
Income taxes (40%)		
Net Income	_____	_____

b. Comment briefly on the changes between the two years.

_____

_____

_____

_____

_____

_____

_____

_____

Chapter 17
Answers to Questions and Exercises

True or False

1.	F	6.	T	11.	F
2.	T	7.	T	12.	T
3.	F	8.	F	13.	T
4.	T	9.	T	14.	T
5.	F	10.	F	15.	F

Multiple Choice

1. b
2. a
3. c
4. a
5. a
6. d

Complete the Statements

1. vertical
2. working capital
3. diluted
4. market
5. 1 − tax rate

6. Financial leverage
7. positive
8. inventory turnover
9. price/earnings
10. horizontal

Exercises

17-1.

a. $\dfrac{\$86,000}{\$40,000} = 2.15 \text{ to } 1$

b. $\dfrac{\$44,000}{\$40,000} = 1.10 \text{ to } 1$

c. $\dfrac{\$100,000}{\$200,000} = 0.5 \text{ to } 1$

d. $\dfrac{\$450,000}{\$36,000} = 12.5 \text{ times (Accounts Receivable Turnover)}$

$\dfrac{365}{\text{Accounts Receivable Turnover}} = \dfrac{365}{12.5} = 29.2 \text{ days}$

e. $\dfrac{\$270,000}{\$40,000} = 6.75 \text{ times}$

f. $\dfrac{\$51,000}{\$6,000} = 8.5 \text{ times}$

g. $\dfrac{\$27,000 + [\$6,000 \times (1 - .40)] = \$30,600}{\left(\dfrac{\$250,000 + \$300,000}{2}\right)} = 11.1\%$

h.

	Beginning of Year	End of Year
Total stockholders' equity	$180,000	$200,000
Less preferred stock	50,000	50,000
Common stockholders' equity	$130,000	$150,000

$$\frac{\$27,000 - (8\% \times \$50,000) = \$23,000}{\left(\dfrac{\$130,000 + \$150,000}{2}\right)} = \underline{16.4\%}$$

i. Financial leverage is positive, since the return on the common stockholders' equity is greater than the return on total assets.

17-2.

	19x5	19x4	19x3	19x2	19x1
Sales	140%	135%	130%	115%	100%
Accounts Receivable	180%	150%	130%	115%	100%

Sales grew by 15 percent per year through 19x3, and then dropped off to a 5 percent growth rate for the next two years. The accounts receivable grew at a 15 percent rate through 19x3, but then rather than dropping off to a 5 percent rate the accounts receivable grew at an even faster rate through 19x5. This suggests that the company is granting credit too liberally, and that large bad debts may soon be encountered.

17-3.

a.

ELDREDGE COMPANY
Common-Size Comparative Income Statements
For the Years Ended December 31, 19x1 and 19x2

	19x2	19x1
Sales	100.0	100.0
Cost of goods sold	70.0	66.2
Gross margin	30.0	33.8
Operating expenses:		
Selling expenses	14.5	14.5
Administrative expenses	7.8	10.2
Total operating expenses	22.3	24.7
Net operating income	7.7	9.1
Interest expense	0.2	0.3
Net income before taxes	7.5	8.8
Income taxes	3.0	3.5
Net Income	4.5	5.3

b. The two primary areas affecting the percentage decrease in net income were cost of goods sold and administrative expenses. Cost of goods sold increased from 66.2 percent of sales in 19x1 to 70.0 percent of sales in 19x2—an increase of 3.8 percentage points. On the other hand, administrative expenses dropped from 10.2 percent of sales in 19x1 to only 7.8 percent of sales in 19x2—a decrease of 2.4 percentage points. The net effect was a decrease in net income as a percentage of sales, which fell from 5.3 percent of sales in 19x1 to only 4.5 percent of sales in 19x2.

Chapter 18

"How Well Am I Doing?"—Statement of Changes in Financial Position

Chapter Study Suggestions

A statement of changes in financial position can be prepared in either of two ways: by analyzing changes in working capital, or by analyzing changes in cash. Accordingly, Chapter 18 is divided into two parts, with the first part focusing on changes in working capital (a "funds" statement) and the second part focusing on changes in cash (a "cash flow" statement).

In the first part of the chapter, carefully study the sections titled, "Sources and Uses of Working Capital" and "Three Basic Steps to the Funds Statement." They hold the key to understanding how a funds statement is constructed. Two examples are given of the actual preparation of a funds statement—one example without the use of working papers, and a more complex example with the use of working papers. *Study each example through step by step*. In the case of the more complex example, trace each journal entry into the working papers contained in Exhibit 18-11. If you do all of this with care, you should have a minimum of difficulty in understanding and using the concepts developed in the first part of the chapter.

The second part of the chapter expands only slightly on the concepts which have already been introduced, by showing how these concepts can be used in preparing a cash flow statement. The key sections here are the ones titled, "What Activities Have an Impact on Cash?," "Sources of Cash," and "Uses of Cash." These sections explain how a cash flow statement differs from a funds statement. Study the working papers given in Exhibit 18-14 with care, noting how they differ from the working papers given earlier in Exhibit 18-11.

CHAPTER HIGHLIGHTS AND STUDY GUIDE

A. The statement of changes in financial position is prepared to show the reasons for changes in a company's working capital position or in its cash position during a period.

1. When changes in working capital are being analyzed, the statement is often called a "funds statement" for brevity. An example of a well prepared funds statement is presented in Exhibit 18-1.

2. When changes in the cash position are being analyzed, the statement is often called a "cash flow statement" for brevity. An example of a well prepared cash flow statement is presented in Exhibit 18-13.

B. There are three basic steps to follow in preparing a funds statement:

1. Find the change which has taken place in working capital during the year.

2. Analyze the change which has taken place in each noncurrent balance sheet account, to determine if the change resulted in a source or a use of working capital.

3. Total the sources and uses of working capital obtained in Step 2. The difference between the total sources and the total uses should equal the change in working capital obtained in Step 1.

C. There are three major sources of working capital in an organization. They are: profitable operations; long-term financing; and sales of plant, equipment, or other noncurrent assets.

1. Profitable operations (net income) represents the most significant continuing source of working capital in most firms.

a. In order to compute the amount of working capital provided by operations it is necessary to add back the depreciation expense deducted on the income statement for the period. The format is:

Sources of working capital:
From operations:

Net income	$XXX
Add: Depreciation	XX
Total from operations	$XXX

b. The reason depreciation must be added back to the net income is that it is an expense which does not require a current outlay of funds. Therefore, in order to convert the income statement data to a funds basis, it is necessary to cancel out the effects of depreciation. This is done by adding depreciation back to the net income figure from which it was previously deducted.

c. Certain other charges on the income statement also reduce net income without involving a current outflow of funds. These charges include depletion of natural resources, deferred income taxes, and amortization of goodwill, patents, and leaseholds. Like depreciation, they must be added back to net income in determining the amount of funds provided by operations during a period.

2. Long-term financing is also a significant source of working capital in most organizations. Long-term financing includes funds obtained from sales of capital stock and issues of long-term debt.

3. Sales of plant, equipment, and various other noncurrent assets represent a third source of working capital in an organization. However, this source is less significant than the other two. Generally, assets are sold only at infrequent intervals.

D. There are four major uses of working capital in an organization. They are: unprofitable operations; retirement of long-term financing; purchases of plant, equipment, and other noncurrent assets; and the declaration of dividends.

1. If operations are unprofitable, then a firm will suffer a net outflow of resources, resulting in a depletion of working capital for the period.

a. However, even if the income statement shows a net loss for the period, the working capital provided by operations can still be positive. This can happen if the net loss is smaller than the depreciation expense which has been deducted for the period. To illustrate:

Net income (loss)....................	$(35,000)
Add: Depreciation	50,000
Total from operations	$ 15,000

b. As this example suggests, the composition of the working capital provided by operations is equally as important as the amount provided.

2. If a firm decides to retire capital stock or long-term debt, then working capital is drained out of the organization as a result of the retirements.

    a. Great care must be taken to be sure that these retirements do not damage the company's working capital position.

    b. Generally, sales and retirements of long-term debt or capital stock will be closely correlated over a period of years. The funds statement offers a method of monitoring this balance of sales and retirements.

3. The purchase of plant, equipment, and other noncurrent assets represents a major use of working capital from year to year.

4. The declaration of cash dividends also represents a major use of working capital. It is the declaration of dividends, rather than the payment of dividends, that has the effect on working capital.

    a. This is because the declaration of dividends increases current liabilities, and thus reduces working capital.

    b. The later payment of a dividend which has already been declared will have no effect on working capital.

E.   To summarize, those transactions which will result in either a source or a use of working capital have a common identifying characteristic: *they involve a change in a noncurrent balance sheet account which also affects a current asset or a current liability account in some way.*

F.   There are two groups of transactions which have no effect on working capital. One group appears on the funds statement, and the other does not.

1. The first group consists of transactions affecting only current asset and current liability accounts. An example would be the collection of an account receivable. Transactions in this group *do not* appear on the funds statement, since they have no effect on *net* working capital.

2. The second group consists of transactions involving only noncurrent balance sheet accounts. An example would be the issue of capital stock for buildings or equipment.

    a. Transactions of this type are called "direct exchange" transactions. Such transactions *do* appear on the fund statement, even though no change in working capital is involved.

    b. The exchange is treated as a "sale" and as a "purchase," with the sale being treated as a source of funds, and the purchase as a use of funds.

G.   The section titled, "The Funds Statement—An Illustration," provides a step-by-step example of the construction of a funds statement. Study this section carefully.

H.   The section titled, "A Working Paper Approach to the Funds Statement," provides an example of how working papers can assist in funds statement preparation.

1. Exhibit 18-11 contains a set of completed working papers. Notice that a T-account is provided for each noncurrent balance sheet account. A T-account is also provided for "Working Capital" in which sources and uses are entered.

2. Each noncurrent account is analyzed, and the entry(s) explaining the change in the account are entered into it, with offsetting entries being made in the working capital T-account.

I.   In preparing a statement of changes in financial position, some firms prefer to focus on cash, rather than to focus on working capital. A statement of this type is sometimes called a "cash flow statement." Its purpose is to explain the cause of any increase or decrease in cash.

1. Sources of cash include:

    a. Profitable operations.

    b. Long-term financing (sales of capital stock or issues of long-term debt).

    c. Sales of plant, equipment, or other noncurrent assets.

    d. An increase in any current liability account.

    e. A decrease in any current asset account.

2. Uses of cash include:

    a. Unprofitable operations.

    b. Retirement of long-term financing (capital stock or long-term debt).

    c. Purchase of plant, equipment, or other noncurrent assets.

    d. A decrease in any current liability account.

    e. An increase in any current asset account.

3. Thus, current asset and current liability accounts must be analyzed, along with noncurrent balance sheet accounts, when a cash flow statement is being prepared. An example of a cash flow statement is given in Exhibit 18-13.

a. Notice how this statement differs from the funds statement given earlier in Exhibit 18-1.

b. Working papers for a cash flow statement are provided in Exhibit 18-14. Notice that these working papers contain changes in the current asset and current liability accounts, as well as changes in the noncurrent balance sheet accounts. Otherwise, the procedure is the same as that illustrated earlier.

Appendix—Modified Cash Flow Statement

A.   When preparing a cash flow statement, some managers prefer a format which adjusts all changes in current assets and current liabilities through the income statement.

1. The procedure for making this adjustment is presented in Exhibit 18-16. Notice that through this adjustment process the income statement is changed to a cash basis.

2. A cash flow statement using this modified format is presented in Exhibit 18-17.

B.   If working papers are used, then the income statement is *automatically* adjusted to a cash basis as part of the working paper procedure. This procedure is illustrated in Exhibit 18-18 in the text.

REVIEW AND SELF TEST
Questions and Exercises

True or False

For each of the following statements, enter a T or an F in the blank to indicate whether the statement is true or false.

_____ 1. The statement of changes in financial position is sometimes referred to as a funds statement.

_____ 2. In order to determine the amount of "Funds Provided by Operations," it is necessary to add back depreciation expense and similar nonfund charges from the income statement.

_____ 3. The sale of equipment would not represent a source of working capital in an organization, since equipment is not a current asset.

_____ 4. If the income statement shows a net loss for a period, then the "Working Capital Provided by Operations" figure cannot be positive.

_____ 5. It is the declaration of cash dividends, rather than the payment of cash dividends, that represents a use of working capital.

_____ 6. The collection of an account receivable would represent a source of working capital in an organization.

_____ 7. If a company is profitable, then working capital will always increase during the year.

_____ 8. Short-term borrowing may be a source of cash, but it is not a source of working capital.

_____ 9. If capital stock is issued in exchange for equipment, then there will be no change in the amount of working capital, but the transaction should appear on the funds statement *as if* both a source and a use of working capital was involved.

_____ 10. A transaction that affects only current assets and current liabilities will leave total working capital unchanged.

_____ 11. Those transactions which will result in either a source or a use of working capital have a common identifying characteristic: they involve a change in a noncurrent balance sheet account which also affects a current asset or a current liability account in some way.

_____ 12. The payment of a previously declared cash dividend represents a use of working capital.

_____ 13. Depreciation represents a major source of working capital in an organization.

_____ 14. In order to determine why working capital increased or decreased during a period, the manager must analyze the noncurrent balance sheet accounts.

_____ 15. In a cash flow statement, an increase in accounts receivable would represent a source of cash.

_____ 16. In a cash flow statement, a decrease in inventory would represent a source of cash.

_____ 17. In a cash flow statement, an increase in a liability account (current or noncurrent) would represent a source of cash.

_____ 18. A cash flow statement does not show changes in noncurrent balance sheet accounts such as capital stock, long-term debt, and plant and equipment.

_____ 19. (Appendix) In order to adjust revenue (as reported on the income statement) to a cash basis, it is necessary to deduct any increase in accounts receivable or to add any decrease in accounts receivable.

_____ 20. (Appendix) In order to adjust cost of goods sold (as reported on the income statement) to a cash basis, it is necessary to adjust the cost of goods sold figure for changes in both inventory and accounts payable.

Multiple Choice

Choose the best answer or response by placing the identifying letter in the space provided.

For Questions 1 through 8 below, indicate whether the item is: a) added to net income to obtain "Working Capital Provided by Operations"; b) deducted from net income to obtain "Working Capital Provided by Operations"; c) a source of working capital separate from net income; d) a use of working capital; e) none of these.

_____ 1. The payment of an account payable due to a creditor.

_____ 2. A $50,000 increase in deferred income taxes.

_____ 3. The retirement of fully depreciated equipment.

_____ 4. The purchase of $100,000 in fixed assets on a 60-day short-term note.

_____ 5. A sale of equipment, for cash, at its book value.

_____ 6. The amortization of goodwill appearing on the income statement.

_____ 7. The declaration of a stock dividend.

_____ 8. The reclassification of $250,000 in long-term debt to a current liability status.

_____ 9. Which of the following is not a use of working capital: a) the repurchase of common stock; b) the purchase of equipment by giving a note due in 90 days; c) the purchase of inventory on account; d) the

repayment of long-term debt; e) all of these are uses of working capital.

_____ 10. (Appendix) Cost of goods sold on the income statement is $50,000. During the year, inventories increased by $12,000 and accounts payable increased by $16,000. The cost of goods sold adjusted to a cash basis would be: a) $46,000; b) $54,000; c) $22,000; d) $78,000; e) none of these.

Complete the Statements

Fill in the necessary words to complete the following statements.

1. The cause of a change in working capital can be determined by analyzing the changes in the _____ balance sheet accounts and determining whether these changes resulted in a _____ or a _____ of working capital.

2. Depreciation and other noncash expenses should be added back to _____ _____ to determine the amount of working capital provided by operations during a period.

3. A transaction which affects only _____ _____ and/or _____ _____ accounts will not change total working capital and hence will not appear on the funds statement.

4. The _____ of a cash dividend is a use of working capital.

5. The most significant source of working capital in most organizations is from _____

6. A statement prepared by management to analyze the sources and uses of cash is called a _____ _____ statement.

7. A decrease in accounts receivable during a period would be a _____ of cash on a cash flow statement.

8. In preparing a cash flow statement, the manager must analyze both _____ and _____ balance sheet accounts.

9. (Appendix) The cash flow from operations can be determined by converting the _____ _____ to a cash basis.

10. (Appendix) Operating expenses can be adjusted to a cash basis by adding any _____ in prepaid expenses and deducting any _____ in accrued liabilities.

Exercises

18-1. Comparative financial statements for Mardex Company are given below:

	19x2	19x1
Current assets:		
Cash	$ 4	$ 10
Accounts receivable, net	30	24
Inventory	45	40
Total	79	74
Buildings and equipment	180	140
Less accumulated depreciation	42	30
Net buildings and equipment	138	110
Land	25	25
Investment in other companies	8	16
Total Assets	$250	$225
Current liabilities:		
Accounts payable	$ 32	$ 30
Bonds payable	40	55
Stockholders' equity:		
Common stock	125	100
Retained earnings	53	40
Total stockholders' equity	178	140
Total Liabilities and Equity	$250	$225
Sales	$425	
Less cost of goods sold	275	
Gross margin	150	
Less operating expenses	130	
Net Income	$ 20	

During 19x2 the company declared and paid $7 in cash dividends. The operating expenses for 19x2 contain $12 in depreciation expense.

a. Prepare an analysis of changes in working capital.

MARDEX COMPANY
Analysis of Changes in Working Capital
For the Year Ended December 31, 19x2

	19x2	19x1	Working Capital Increase (decrease)
Current assets:			
Total			
Current liabilities:			
Total			
Working Capital			

b.   Prepare a funds statement in good form. Working papers are not necessary.

MARDEX COMPANY
Statement of Changes in Financial Position
For the Year Ended December 31, 19x2

Sources of Working Capital:

Total sources .... ‗‗‗‗‗

Uses of Working Capital:

Total uses .... ‗‗‗‗‗

_____ in Working Capital..................... ‗‗‗‗‗

18-2. Refer to the financial statement data for Mardex Company contained in the preceding exercise. The president of Mardex is confused as to why cash decreased during 19x2, since the company had a strong net income showing for the year. Prepare a cash flow statement for the year. It is not necessary to prepare working papers.

MARDEX COMPANY
Statement of Changes in Financial Position
For the Year Ended December 31, 19x2

Sources of Cash:

Total sources .... ‗‗‗‗‗

Uses of Cash:

Total uses .... ‗‗‗‗‗

_____ in Cash .... ‗‗‗‗‗

18-3. (Appendix) Balance sheet account data for Ingalls Company follow:

	19x5	19x4
Cash	$ 6	$ 10
Accounts receivable, net	20	14
Inventory	60	48
Prepaid expenses	3	6
Buildings and equipment	175	150
Accumulated depreciation	(52)	(40)
Investments in other companies	8	12
Total Assets	$220	$200
Accounts payable	$ 42	$ 35
Accrued liabilities	8	15
Bonds payable	40	25
Common stock	100	115
Retained earnings	30	10
Total Liabilities and Equity	$220	$200

Income statement data for 19x5 follow:

Sales	$350
Cost of goods sold	225
Gross margin	125
Less operating expenses	100
Net Income	$ 25

During 19x5 the company declared and paid $5 in cash dividends. Depreciation expense of $12 is included in the 19x5 operating expenses above.

a.   Prepare a schedule adjusting the company's income to a cash basis:

Sales $350
Adjustments to a cash basis:

Sales adjusted to a cash basis .... $
Cost of goods sold $225
Adjustments to a cash basis:

Cost of goods sold adjusted to a cash basis .... $
Operating expenses $100
Adjustments to a cash basis:

Operating expenses adjusted to a cash basis .... $
Net Cash Flow From Operations ....

b.   Prepare a cash flow statement in good form:

INGALLS COMPANY
Statement of Changes in Financial Position
For the Year Ended December 31, 19x5

Sources of Cash:

Total sources .... ‾‾‾‾‾

Uses of Cash:

Total uses .... ‾‾‾‾‾
_____ in Cash .... $‾‾‾‾‾

Chapter 18
Answers to Questions and Exercises

True or False

1. T	8. T	15. F
2. T	9. T	16. T
3. F	10. T	17. T
4. F	11. T	18. F
5. T	12. F	19. T
6. F	13. F	20. T
7. F	14. T	

Multiple Choice

1. e	6. a
2. a	7. e
3. e	8. d
4. d	9. c
5. c	10. a

Complete the Statements

1. noncurrent, source, use
2. net income
3. current asset, current liability
4. declaration
5. operations
6. cash flow
7. source
8. current, noncurrent
9. income statement
10. increase, increase

Exercises

18-1. a.

	19x2	19x1	Working Capital Increase (decrease)
Current assets:			
Cash	$ 4	$10	$(6)
Accounts receivable, net	30	24	6
Inventory	45	40	5
Total	79	74	5
Current liabilities:			
Accounts payable	32	30	(2)
Working Capital	$47	$44	$ 3

b. Sources of working capital:

Operations:

Net income	$20
Add back expenses not requiring the use of working capital:	
Depreciation	12
Total from operations	32
Sale of investments	8
Sale of common stock	25
Total sources	65

Uses of working capital:

Purchase of buildings and equipment	40
Retirement of bonds payable	15
Cash dividends	7
Total uses	62
Increase in working capital	$ 3

18-2. Sources of cash:

Operations:

Net income	$20
Add back expenses not requiring the use of working capital:	
Depreciation	12
Total from operations	32
Sale of investments	8
Increase in accounts payable	2
Sale of common stock	25
Total sources	67

Uses of cash:

Increase in accounts receivable	6
Increase in inventory	5
Purchase of buildings and equipment	40
Retirement of bonds payable	15
Cash dividends	7
Total uses	73
Decrease in cash	$ (6)

18-3. **a.**

Sales	$350	
Adjustments to a cash basis:		
Deduct increase in accounts receivable	− 6	
Sales adjusted to a cash basis		$344
Cost of goods sold	$225	
Adjustments to a cash basis:		
Add increase in inventory	+12	
Deduct increase in accounts payable	− 7	
Cost of goods sold adjusted to a cash basis		230
Operating expenses..	$100	
Adjustments to a cash basis:		
Deduct decrease in prepaid expenses	− 3	
Add decrease in accrued liabilities	+ 7	
Deduct depreciation expense	−12	
Operating expenses adjusted to a cash basis		92
Net Cash Flow from Operations		$ 22

b. Sources of cash:

Net cash flow from operations	$ 22
Sale of investments..	4
Issue of bonds payable...	15
Total sources...	41

Uses of cash:

Purchase of buildings and equipment	25
Retirement of common stock	15
Cash dividends	5
Total uses...	45
Decrease in cash	$ (4)